LEADERSHIP WITH GOAT HEAD

Moving From Godless to Godly Leadership

LEADERSHIP WITH GOAT HEAD

Moving From Godless to Godly Leadership

Prof. John Gatungu Githiga

All Nations Christ Church International
Copyright © 2021 by Prof. John Gatungu Githiga.

All rights reserved. No part of this book may be reproduced in any form or by any electronic or mechanical means, including information storage and retrieval systems, without permission in writing from the publisher, except by reviewers, who may quote brief passages in a review.

ISBN: 978-1-957054-27-8 (Paperback Edition)
ISBN: 978-1-957054-28-5 (Hardcover Edition)
ISBN: 978-1-957054-26-1 (E-book Edition)

Library of Congress Control Number: 2021924520

Book Ordering Information

Phone Number: 315 288-7939 ext. 1000 or 347-901-4920
Email: info@globalsummithouse.com
Global Summit House
www.globalsummithouse.com

Printed in the United States of America

Contents

About The Book 11
Acknowledgement 13
Dedication 15
Leadership With Goat Head..1
Proffesor With Goat Head...5
Each One Teach One 7
Students With Good Shepherd Heart.....................................11
Shepherding And Pastoral Visits 13
Shepherding And Reconciliation 23
Bishops With Goat Head 25
Departure From The Episcopal Church.................................33
President Mary And The Good Shepherd 39
Do You Speak English?..43
The Good Shepherd In Zoe Church 47
The Good Shepherd And Victory 49
Political Leaders With Goat Head 51
Kings With Goat Head 57
Political Leaders With The Good Shepherd 59
A Shephered At The Edge Of A Cliff......................................61
Consecration Of The Bishops..79
We Give What We Have Received..83
A Shepherd Dreamed Carring
An Elephant..89
Sheperding In Sudan 103
Mission And The Cross 113
Shepherding In Spite Of Criticisms 119
Christ At The Center..123
Nurture Your Best Self..125
Fighting A Good Fight 129
Conclusion..139

LEADERSHIP WITH GOAT HEAD
Moving From Godless to Godly Leadership

OTHER BOOKS BY THE AUTHOR

The Spirit in the Black Soul
CHRIST AND ROOTS: Jesus as Revealed in the Bible and the African Traditional Religions
THE HOLY SPIRIT: The Greatest Promise and the Greatest Gift of All
INITIATION AND PASTORAL PSYCHOLOGY: Toward African Personality Theory
MINISTRY TO ALL NATIONS: Practical Theology of Mission and Church Planting
70 SERMONS: Liturgical Preaching
GOSPEL TO ALL NATIONS: Preaching from the Lectionary
THE SECRETS OF SUCCESS IN MARRIAGE
25 SECRETS OF SUCCESS IN MARRIAGE
30 SECREATS OF SUCCESS IN MARRIAGE: A Book for Premarital and Marriage Counseling
SYSTEMATIC THEOLOGY: An Introduction to the African Theological Voice
FROM VICTORY TO VICTORY
FRUITFUL FAMILY: Family Therapy Based on Christian Principles
DAILY DEVOTION FOR THE NATIONS
THE HOLY TRINITY AND US: *Viewing the Holy Trinity from Practical Theology Perspective*

Professor John G Githiga is Patriarch of All Nations Christ Church International which is association of churches and ministry with the presence in every continent and founder, Chancellor and CEO of ANCCI University which is interdenominational and international. He is former Chaplain and faculty at West Texas A&M University where he taught Biblical studies and was President of United Campus Ministries. He is former chaplain and lecturer at Grambling State University where he taught Swahili and African philosophy and started KWANZA celebration. He was instructor at Pensacola Junior College where he taught in the department Humanity. He lectured on humanity in ancient world. Humanity and art and humanity and technological society. He was the head of the Department of Pastoral Theology at St. Paul's University (Kenya) where he taught pastoral theology and human background to pastoral ministry. He is founder and first president of the African Association for Pastoral Study and Counselling. He presided over Congress on Pastoral studies which were held at Democratic Republic of Congo. He is a graduate from Church Army College, St. Paul's United Theological College, Maker ere University, the University of the South, Vanderbilt University and the International Bible Institute and Seminary. He holds a Diploma of Theology, Master of Divinity, Doctor of Ministry, Doctor of Religious Education, Doctor of Divinity. He is a student of theology, sociology, psychology, cultural anthropology and humanity. He was featured in the 2008-2009 edition of Madison Who's who in Executives and Professionals having demonstrated exemplary achievement and made distinguished contributions to the business community. He received certificate of recognition as the Donor of the year 2021 from United State Deputy Sheriff's and the Paralyzed Veteran of America. He is married to the Rev. Dr. Mary Githiga.

ABOUT THE BOOK

This book is intended to encourage the faithful ministers of the Gospel who are suffering from ungodly leaders. It intends to encourage them because God who has called them is the Almighty and faithful judge and the Great Provider. The author share with reader how God is the present help in the time of trouble. It shows the importance of spiritual partners, daily devotion, being in Christ so as to bear the fruits of the Spirit and of having mission statement. It also call the leaders with goat head to commit themselves Christ as Paul did-The persecutor of the church turned to God and became an Apostle. It also reveals how the author used challenges as stepping stones to hinger achievement which led him to being, Patriarch of All Nations Christian Church International, Chancellor of ANCCI University and founder President of ANCCI Institute

ACKNOWLEDGEMENT

We are most grateful to all who have supported the ministry which God has given us with prayer and financial contribution. This includes Dr David Brister, Rev Dr Elizabeth and Dr Alan Larson, Mr. Neil Crick. Mrs. Sally Harris, Rehema Githiga, Isaac Githiga and my beloved wife, The Rev Dr Mary Githiga. May God richly bless you

DEDICATION

This book is dedicated to all those who serve God in the power of the Holy Spirit and all those who paid the ultimate prize for their faithfulness in ministry. To my father and mother Isaac Githiga and Joyce Njeri Githiga and my father-in-law and mother-in-law Hiram and Joyce Wambui Kahungu.

CHAPTER ONE

LEADERSHIP WITH GOAT HEAD

It is very interest to examine two types of leadership and shepherding-the leadership with goat head and the leadership with the heart of the Good Shepherd. There are those leaders with permanent goat head and those with temporary goat attitudes but when they repent, they replace the goat head with shepherd heart. In Matthew 25:31-46. Defines those with parment goat head as those who will be on the lift side and the King will say to them:

"Depart from me you who are cursed, into the eternal fire prepared for devil and his angels. For I was hungry and you gave me nothing to eat, I was thirsty and you gave me nothing to drink, I was a stranger and you did not welcome me, I needed cloth and you did not cloth me, I was sick and in prison and you did not look after me." and when they answered:

"Lord, when did we see you hungry or thirsty or stranger or needing cloth or in prison, and did not help you."

"He will reply, 'I tell you the truth, whatever you did not do for the least of these, you did not do for me.' Then they will go away to eternal punishment."

To those with the shepherd heart he will say:

"Come you who are blessed by my Father take your inheritance. For I was hungry and you gave me something to eat, I was thirsty and you gave me some water to drink, I was a stranger and you invited me in, I needed clothing and you cloth me, I was sick and you looked after me, I was in prison and you came to visit me."

They of cause did this because the Good Shepherd was in their heart not because of what they could get in return. This is why they asked the King:

"When did we see you hungry and feed you, or thirsty and gave you something to drink? When did we see you a stranger and invited you in or needing cloth and clothe you? When did we see you sick or in prison and to visit you? Then the King answered: whatever you did to the one of the least of these brothers, you did for me."

The Bible give us the precise character of the religious and political leaders without the Good Shepherd: St Paul summarizes their characteristics this way: "the act of sinful nature is are obvious: sexual immorality, impurity and debauchery, idolatry and witchcraft; hatred, discord, jealousy, fits of rage, selfish ambition, dissensions, factions and envy drunkenness, orgies, and the like. I warn you as I did before, those who live like this will not inherit the kingdom of God." This group is not actually in the kingdom of God. They don't have the Holy Spirit.

Those who are in Christ bear the fruits of the Holy Spirit which is: "love, joy, patience, kindness goodness, faithfulness, gentleness and self-control." All what we need to bear this fruit is to be in Christ: This is what he says: "I am the vine; you are the branches. If a man remains in me and I in him, he will bear much fruit, apart from me you can do nothing." John 15:5.

However, it has to be pointed out that Christians cannot commit sin. In the gospel, while Jesus was talking about his suffering. He said: "the son of man will be betrayed into the hands of men. They will kill him, and after three days he will rise." Mark 9: 31. While he was talking about his suffering John and James were concern about power. They wanted one of them to be vice President and the other the Secretary of State. They were concern about who will be the greatest in the Kingdom of God. Jesus responded with: "If anyone wants to be first, he must be the very last, and the servant of all." Mark 9:35. Even after Jesus advice they bilged: "Teach, said John, we saw a man driving daemon in your name and we told him to stop, because he was not one of us." To this Jesus responded: Do not stop him… no one who does miracle by my name can in the next moment say anything bad about me. For whoever is not against us is for us. I tell you the truth anyone who give you cup of water in my name because you belong to Christ will certainly lose his reward." Mark 9:39-41.

Like my name's sake John, I have found myself suffering from temporary goat head. I had this experience when I was writing a book of THE HOLY TRINITY AND US. The episode reminded me about my professors who had similar experience

CHAPTER TWO

PROFFESOR WITH GOAT HEAD

—⁓∾⊙⊱⊙⊰⊙⊱⊙∾⁓—

I had a real challenge when I was commanded to write a book about God who has revealed himself as one in three. After humbling myself and became obedient, I had abundance of vision about the subject. But going half way my mind became blank and the flow of vision halted. I then remembered the word of our Lord: "whoever wants to be great must become the servant of all." So, I decided to be obedient and started the day by going to the Walmart to get the glossers for the family. In the store a white lady noted that I have more fruits than other Items. She looked at me and said: "You have lot of fruits. I must start eating more fruits." Looking at pawpaw, she asked me: "How do you prepare this?" I replied: "you just peal it cut slices and eat it." "So, you don't have to cook it?" responded the lady. "No, you don't cook it." I responded. Going to my car, I found a small paper on my widescreen with a message: "Bro learn how to park." I then realized that I had also double parked. Thus, I agreed with my brother, I need to learn how to park.

After this I returned home and prepared breakfast for my dear wife. When I was halfway Mary was up and we started preparing the breakfasts together. We reminded ourselves our kitchen mission statement: "By love, serve one another." This was the theme of the last sermon of our British spiritual father Rev Martin Pepiatt. He preached this sermon when we were youth at St Christopher Church, Nakuru. And so normally, I prepare fruits, while Mary prepares tea and cereal or oatmeal. When we were enjoying our breakfast, we gratefully remembered Father Martin. In the process, the professor head was restored. And I had abundance of vision about the Holy Trinity.

CHAPTER THREE

EACH ONE TEACH ONE

—⁂—

The above episode reminded me of several critical incidents which I faced when I was a student in the University of the South. It so happened that I was the only black student in the class. On my second year I had a call to start ministry among African American. We decided that we will call the group each on teach one. I need to learn from them as they also learned from me. One of the challenges which I faced was that the only Black person who could take me around was a woman. And whoever we found a man in the house, he would not participate in discussion. And even when we form a group, men in attendance didn't participate and those who tried to participate were shouted down by the ladies. However, the group grew in number. In winter, we agreed that if there was lot snow, we will have no meeting. The critical episode took place the day after calling the meeting off. It took place in the class which was led by the student. The theme was: "They (Black) don't get the bread because we have tied their hands. The professor who was seating on my right hand stared a fight before the class started. He asked: "Githiga, why didn't attend you group last night?" "How did you get that information?" "From Helen (she was his domestic servant). Before I had to answer the question; he said: "You did not attend the class because of that dump car. That dump care will take you to hell." I then responded: "If my dump care will take me to hell, why didn't you give me your car which will take to heaven?" At this point the students who were leading the class said: "time to start." The theme of subject was: "They (black) don't get the bread because we have tied their hands." They had prepared a skit. They have put bread on the table and a roap. They ask us to tie the hands of the person on our right and then the pair will run to pick up the bread. The professor happens to be on my right and was smaller than I. With bitterness I help his hands and tied them tightly as I use to tie a fighting cow when milking. The prof shouted: "Githiga you are hurting me!" After tying his hands, we had to run to the table to grumble the bread. And so, I got the bread. After this we were asked to say what we felt. My quick respond was: "I felt so good when Jack was yielding because unless the hands of the people like him are tied, we will never get the bread. Of cause what happened between the Prof and I exceeded the expectation the class leaders.

In the afternoon we have to meet in a core group which was a group of seven students and a faculty which was reflecting on what was going on with students. This group was every useful and educative. The issue of Githiga the professor was brought up. I thought everybody was on my side but I was wrong. The professor who was with us said: "The problem is about how you got the money for buying the car. We suspect that the CIA has given you money because they needed to get some information from you." To this I responded: "I really cannot understand your concept of God. If the loving Father can give each of your families two cars, why is he incapable of providing the Githiga family with one car?" There was no comment.

When I share in incident with "EACH ONE TEACH ONE." I was informed that they don't take their best car to the place of work. They normally have two cars. The one which look like a junk is the one they drove to work. From the group I learned the importance of claiming the inner liberty which is well at curate by Stephen Biko, the father of black theology. He wrote: "the sense of defeat is what we are fighting against. People must not just give in to the hardships of life. People must develop a hope. People must develop some form of security to be together and to look at their problems. And people must in this way, build up their humanity. This is the point about Black Consciousness."

The other challenged I face from Prof of the Old Testament. The OT course had 10 credit hours and was requisite for Master of Divinity program. The prof believed that no primitive person can make it in his course. The African student who was before me took the class when this prof was on sabbatical leave. When he returned, he told my fellow student: "you were very lack you did it when I was away. Otherwise, I don't think you could make it." When he was teaching, if could raise my hand to ask a question, he never responded. But whenever he was discussing something which he thought it was primitive. He will ask: "let us get the view of the primitive man." This was indeed disgusting. Whatever paper I wrote I was given F. Consequently, I had to take him to the Dean. To my greatest surprise, when I ask him why I am only getting F in his class while in all other classes I get B+ and A; He responded: "John, have ever gotten angry since you came here? " I responded: "What has anger to do with the Old Testament.?" This ended our meeting. The Dean who was Professor of theology and cultural Anthropology noted the problem and he gave me another prof to teach me the OT. I had a blessing of being taught by one teacher for semester and I got the passing grade.

The challenge I got with OT Prof motivated me for higher achievement. By the time I was finishing the Master's program, I had started doctorate program and within three years I had three doctoral degrees. I used to have two study rooms-one at home and the other at university library. One was called Doctor of Ministry and the other Doctor of Religious Education. When I completed the two programs, I was awarded Doctor of Divinity for the Ministries which I started and was still performing. All glory to God.

The message here is that when people tell you: "You can't." shout to yourself: "Yes we can!" This was mission statement of President Baraka Obama. His antagonist not only said that he can't but he also said that he was not born in America by By shouting: " Yes we can" used he was summoning his triple heritage- Anglo, Kenyan and Indonesian. As you have seen, the reason why we enjoy being Parents of All Nations Christian Church International is because Mary and I have received from many nations Thus, my beloved, the more you received from many nations, and the more you enlarge your ego. We give what we have received.

However, the good news is that there were students and faculty who had the heart of the Good Shepherd. These shepherds arranged that the African student be give an American student who will be helping the student with accent and the student has to be an average student who will not intimidate the African student. I was given Jay (not the actual name). I was asking him to proofread my papers. There was also faculty with the heart of the good shepherd. In the second semester we embarked on New Testament. I was jubilant when the prof of the New Testament asked my mentor in the class: "Jay, are you the one who helped Githiga with his paper." "Yes Sir." Then the Professor responded; "For your information, Githiga has A and you have B." Hence Jay refused be my mentor anymore.

There were other students and faculty with the heart of the good shepherd. At one time Bill Graham, when he was asked after his retirement: "If you would do it all over again, how would you do it?" his answer was: I would study cultural anthropology." The Dean, who had given me full scholarship, was cultural anthropologist. Not only that he was the first to admit African and Asian students, but he uses to invite us and entertain us with our families at his home. He also went to Kenya, and return with good news: "John, you didn't tell me that Kenya is so advanced. " The students with the shepherd heart took us to their home during the holiday and the loving father used us in breaking cultural barriers. To these faculty and students, we are most grateful. One of these students who was a member of Sister of St Mary, became our spiritual partner. And eventually, Mary and I became associates of St Mary. As I write, we give our contribution to the sisters of St Mary.

Hence, my beloved reader, if you have a goat head, all what you need to do is to invite Jesus, the Good Shepherd in your life: He says: "Here am I! I stand at the door and knock. If anyone hears my voice and opens the door, I will come in and eat with him, and he with me."

CHAPTER FOUR

STUDENTS WITH GOOD SHEPHERD HEART

I woke up at 5 am of September 13, 2021 to finish the above chapter. I then went back to bed at 7 am. I had a big dream in which I saw Mabur, our spiritual son and ANCCI University alumni. He came all the way to the kitchen to wash dishes. As he was washing, he broke the handle of the frying pan. When he was doing that, I found myself with corn flower in a bow. I poured some water in it and tasted. To my greatest surprise, it tested sweet. I then said: "I never thought that you can eat corn flower raw."

On Sunday 9.5. 2021 we had worshipped in African Community Church which is pastor by Rev Mabur. They had family Service Sunday and I was one of the speakers. Mabur spoke so highly about Bishop John and Mama Mary. He praised Mary for her hospitality. He said how the bishops sit in the living room talking with the guest while Mama Mary is preparing tea. And how he visited a family where he found woman was the one who was in the living room and the man was the one who was in the Kitchen. He never returns to that home again. After the Service Mrs. Mabur was empathetic to Mary and looking at her, she asked: "are you OK Mama Mary" These few words meant a lot to Mary who at this time was having problem with her lower denture. Also due to chronophobia we stayed a whole year without a visitor. She became leanly and at time she prepared four cups of tea and asked me: "Where are the other persons?" "It is only you and me my dear."

I responded. On addition to powerful message from Mabur the congregation bought our books worthy $800.00 and Mama Mary was given food for a week.

Now, humorously, in the dream, Rev Mabur is the one who is in the Kitchen But both him and the bishop don't seem to know how to function in the kitchen.

After this I open the message in my phone. He wrote: "I really appreciated you coming on Sunday. Your contribution to our conference was highly effective. I will try to find some member who would be vising you to see if there is anything that needs to be done for you. It is time for us to look after you. If you have any need do not hastate to give me a call. I will come right away for you. I am available 4.00 pm to 9.00pm.

This is indeed a letter from a Pastor who has the Spirit of the Good Shepherd.

He is also a son who is following the foot step of his spiritual father. When we were planting the church in Amarillo, we visited international and interfaith families as you will read in the following chapter.

CHAPTER FIVE

SHEPHERDING AND PASTORAL VISITS

Reaching Out to the Muslim Families

On January 11, 2003, the Spirit led us to the Muslim families. We started with Ibrahim's family. They have attended Extravaganza several times. We have also attended a party in their home. They own a middle-class home and have three vehicles.

We were warmly welcomed. Ibrahim was not home, but the mother and her three children were there. It was very noisy as the TV's volume was high . A four-year-old boy had earphones from a CD player plugged in his ears. He was hyper and aggressive. He held two remote controls. With one he controlled his TV and with the other the TV in the living room. Takwa, the twelve-year-old, first-born daughter sat with me and showed me a family album, while Mary was talking with the mother. I asked Takwa to lower the volume of the TV and she obeyed. Mary had carried candies for the children, but before she gave the candies, the mother gave us candies and soda. But we both opted to drink water.

From the family photo we learned that the family is of three worlds. North Sudan is their first world and Lebanon is their second. They resided in Lebanon for five years before proceeding to the United States. At home they speak Arabic. While Ibrahim speaks in the vernacular, Hayawed speaks Arabic and "a little English." Her two daughters are fluent in English and Arabic. Ahmad speaks a mixture of English and Arabic. He doesn't express himself well in any of these languages and this makes him very aggressive. We also observed that Ibrahim was a Sudanese policeman while Hayawed was an actor.

Every member of the family has high self-esteem. Takwa wants to become a medical doctor while her sister Fatima wants to be an actor. The mother hopes for a four-bedroom house so that each child may have her/his own bedroom. She thinks this would reduce sibling fighting. After staying for 45 minutes, we stood and I told them that we needed to go. Hayawed told us that she had called Ibrahim and that we have to wait for him. After waiting for 15 minutes, we bid them farewell. We headed to the Surrs.

As we were pulling into the parking lot of the apartment, we saw Fred and Fatuma driving behind us and we waited for them. Fred is a Congolese and Fatuma is Senegalese. They were speaking in French. No sooner had they alighted than we greeted them. I spoke with Fred while Mary talked with Fatuma. I was conversing in Swahili. Turning to Fatuma, I spoke to her in the same language, not realizing that she doesn't speak Swahili. She looked apprehensive. For a while I didn't understand why she was not responding. Then it dawned on me that I was using a language that was as Greek to Fatuma. I then apologized and I talked to her in English. She invited us to her apartment. Fred bid us farewell.

Entering the house, we found everything was scattered in the living room. She apologized and told us that she has a two-and-half-year-old who jumps everywhere and scatters everything around. We told her that we had a boy who did the same thing. Coumba, who is ten, helped her mom clear the room. As soon as we sat, Fatuma brought us large glasses of orange juice. It seems that Africans have one common heritage: generosity. They are the most generous creatures that God has made.

As we were talking, Abdualaye came in wearing traditional African attire. We expressed great admiration for the outfit. Fatuma then told us that she had made it. She then brought some clothes that she had made. She said she wished to move to a place where there are more Africans who would buy her clothes. Mary, who has a great gift for details, started asking them about the family. They told us that they have six children. Their daughter and son are working at IBP and reside in their own apartment.

"But they are very lazy," complains the father. "They work at night for eight hours and they sleep the whole day while I work overtime and go to school full-time. Most of the time I have only two hours of sleep." "It takes a village to rear a child," I commented.

This was where we needed to step in. Mary praised their daughter. "She is so beautiful. She can be a modelist." After a long conversation we asked them whether they would like to join us for regular worship in the church. They told us that they attend mosque and that they are expected to pray five times a day. But they were sorry to miss our Christmas celebration. They were given wrong directions and for that reason they could not find the church. Now they know where the church is and will be attending Extravaganza.

In the course of our conversation, we learned that Abdulaye is a Tunisian while Fatuma is a Senegalese. In Tunisia the Africans have suffered at the hand of the Arabs. The challenge facing this family is that Fatuma has type 1 diabetes. She takes two insulin shots every day and is pregnant. Because of this, she is not working but has a small income for her disability. Yet the family is confident that things will be better. After visiting with them for fifty minutes we told them we had to go. They persuaded us to stay a bit longer. We insisted that we had to go. Even though it was very cold, Abdulaye escorted us to our car. We felt a bond with this family. We praised God for connecting us to this family.

Two months after this visit, Mohamed, the fifteen-year-old son of Abdulaye, came to church with David, Mary Kenyi's son. He came for healing. He had a constant headache. Hence, I asked him to come forward to the altar. Kneeling down I prayed for him and he was healed. He became connected to the church.

On March 7, 2003, I visited Muslim families. This time Mary was too tired to visit with me. I started with the Abdulaye family. Cumba opened the door and then hid behind the door. Fatuma was lying on the couch very pregnant. She was delighted to see me. After the greetings she asked, "Where is your wife? "She has been very busy today and was too tired to come with me," I responded. "How have you been?" "I am tired," she responded. "My doctor told me that I should be having the baby in three weeks. I have lost my appetite because I have to have two insulin shots every day for diabetes. I also check my blood sugar twice."

As we were talking, three-year-old Ibrahim started climbing the chair. I asked him to come and give me a hug. After a hug he wanted to play ball with me. Then I asked Cumba about her school. She told me that she loves all her teachers. She also likes all the subjects. Her Mom informed me that Cumba, Ayak, and Nono were interviewed on TV yesterday. I was very proud of the family. After twenty minutes I asked them to pray with me. We held our hands together and prayed. I felt a great peace emanating from the Unitive Being.

After this I headed to Sadiq's family. After knocking at the door, Hayawed came to answer the door. She was delighted to see me. "Where's Mary?" she queried. I told her that Mary had a long day and for that reason she was unable to come with me. "Everybody is busy," she generalized. She then gave me a seat. She was watching a story on the Arabic channel. I told her how I would like to speak Arabic and that if it were not for the alphabet, I would learn it easily because Swahili has some commonality with Arabic. She said, "Yes, some similar words include salamu and shetani." After visiting with her I informed her about the forthcoming Gospel Extravaganza, and then we parted. I now headed to the Mexican family of Jorge & Maria Teresa Gonzales.

A Visit to the Mexican Family

This is the first visit to this family. I knocked on the door but nobody answered. I went to the backyard and saw Maria leashing a dog. When she saw me, she welcomed me in the house, the house was well kept. There were flowers on the coffee table with six candles. I commended her for the neatness of her house. She then showed me their wedding photo and the family picture. She has nine sisters and five brothers. Her father is seventy-two and the mother is sixty-five. While she was showing me the pictures Jorge came from the bedroom. After a greeting he said, "Father, we have been waiting for you since 3:00 p.m."

"But I told you that I was coming at 5:00 p.m. I am sorry for keeping you waiting," I apologized. "It is okay, Father," he spoke forgivingly. He then gave me his family photo, which included him, Rocio, and his younger sister. He told me that they are the only three in the family. Unlike Maria, he didn't talk about his father and mother.

"How many children are you planning to have?"

"No more than three," Maria answered emphatically.

"But you are fourteen in your family,' I commented jokingly.

"But none of my brothers or sisters has more than three."

"Tell me about your wedding."

Jorge told me that they were married seven years ago and he does not remember the name of the priest who solemnized their marriage. But they married in a Roman Catholic Church since Maria is a Catholic. "But I like your church," responded Maria. "We would like to be members." I then led them in a discussion about the similarities and differences between the two traditions. A similarity included the holy orders: bishop, priest, and deacon, and the liturgy. I then talked more about the strength of the Anglican Church that it rested on three pillars: tradition, scripture, and reason. I then asked them whether they had a Bible. Maria brought two Bibles to me. One was the Revised Standard Version; the other was a Spanish Bible. Both had pictures and appeared to be children's Bibles. George asked me whether I would get them a Spanish Bible. I told him that I would try to get them one.

I then talked about St. Cyprian's and the Sunday school program, which uses the Catechesis of the Good Shepherd. Jorge interrupted proudly and said, "I don't need someone to teach my children catechism. I can do that myself."

I then explained to him about the program and told him that it takes a village to rear a child. "You cannot do it alone."

Maria then brought up the subject about her children receiving communion. "When we are taking communion, we are taking the body and the blood of Jesus." She said this in Spanish while her husband was interpreting. "A child cannot understand this. I wouldn't like my children to take communion until they are nine." I then told her that was okay.

After that Jorge told me that he would like to do something in the church but is limited because he doesn't speak English well. I subsequently told him that most of our members are learning English and that when he becomes a member, I will give him something to do. After that he told me that he values his children so much that his wife has to stay at home and take care of them. "I always tell my sister that you cannot depend on the day care to take care of your children." I commended him for this but I didn't want to comment about Rocio who is a black sheep in the family.

After the fruitful visit, I bid them farewell. As I pulled away, I was hearing two voices. One was a high voice, the other a low voice. The high voice told me that I needed to visit Rocio as well. The low voice told me that I have done enough for the day and that I was tired. But I opted to listen to the higher voice.

Knocking at the door I was warmly received by the children. It seems that I am the most cherished member of the family. Zeus, a four-year-old son, started playing with his fingers, as I played with mine. Rocio asked me whether I would like to drink something, coffee, apple juice, or water. I preferred apple juice. Zeus, one of the most handsome boys under the sun, looked at me lovingly while holding an orange. "Would like an orange?" "No, thank you." The love and hospitality that I am accorded is replenishing my body and spirit. Rocio looked depressed. She pulled over the chair and sat near the sink.

She was ready to tell me about the fight she had with Carlos, a fight that resulted in the cancellation of the blessing of their marriage. "Father," she started narrating the incident, "I was talking about my nephew. I said that he is beautiful. Then Carlos got angry with me and spit on me. I then hit him with a frying pan. After the fight he left and didn't come back till six in the morning."

"Have you ever stayed for a month without a fight?" I queried.

"No." "Is he still with you? "Yes, but we don't talk to each other. When he is in the house I go to the back yard. When he comes to the backyard, I come to the house. I am not going to live with him. He works twelve hours a day for seven days and then lies to me that he gets only $100. He is supposed to pay the water bill, but has not done so and I am afraid that the city is going to cut off the water. I have so many unpaid bills, and Carlos says that he cannot pay them because they are in my name. The reason is because he doesn't have legal documents. [This means that he is an illegal immigrant.] I am tired of him giving excuses that he cannot pay the bills because they are in my name. I am tired and angry with him for spitting on my children and me." The tears were rolling on her cheeks.

I am also perturbed for the lack of any easy answer. I told her that they both have to learn to live together. After listening to her and giving her words of encouragement, I call the whole family for prayer. We held hands together. As I was praying, Zeus repeated after me while Rocio was sobbing with tears. After the prayer, Misty looked straight in her mother's eye and said, "Don't cry, mom. I love you." She then kissed her mother lovingly and hugged her. I indeed saw the face of Jesus on the face of this child. I then bid them farewell and drove home. I arrived home at 7:30 p.m.

Pastoral Visit to the Dying

March 19, 2003, It was cold, wet, and windy. Mary and I were paying pastoral visits. The previous night Mary was on duty at the Palo Doro Retirement Village, where she worked from 2:00 a.m. to 8:00 a.m. She returned home at 8:15 a.m., went to bed at 9:00 a.m. and slept until noon. I was astonished at her willingness to accompany me for pastoral visits. What dedication! Being on a hospice pastoral team, she had to make a pastoral visit to Sarah (this is not her real name), an Indian woman whose deceased husband was a medical doctor. This productive and ailing mother has five children, all of whom were doctors. This Christian lady had lived in Tanzania, and for that reason she speaks Swahili. Mary is the only person on the hospice team who speaks Swahili.

It was raining when we pulled into her driveway. Mary left me in the car and went to minister to her. After twenty minutes she came back more peaceful and joyous. They had prayed together and recited the verse that Sarah had learned as a child: "For God so

loved the world that He gave his only son, that whosoever believed in him should not perish but have eternal life." John 3:16. They also sang:
Jesus lover of my soul;
Let me to Thy bosom fly.

After this we drove to Fatuma's place. On the way Mary insisted that we go to the store to buy presents for the newly born. We drove to the Dollar General only to discover that neither of us had money and the store didn't take credit cards. Mary remembered that she had her checkbook in her purse. I rushed for it when it started raining on me. We bought the presents and drove to the Surr's home. Fatuma was jubilant when she saw us. She Said: "I called your home several times on Monday but there was no response! I wanted to tell you the good news. That after you came here last Friday and prayed for me. I told him that I was expecting to deliver in three weeks, but the baby came three days after your visit. I had a safe delivery."

We told her that the telephone might have been off the hook. A few minutes later Abulaye came. We asked Fatuma to bring the baby. Holding a handsome 8.5-pound baby boy fueled our joy. His name is Ahamad. "He had lot of hair, but we cut it," Fatuma said. "According to our custom, we believe that birth hair is a bad omen." Then we discussed the naming system. According to Muslims, boys are named after the prophets. That is why we have many men who are named Musa, Ibrahim, and Mohamed, etc. Before we departed Fatuma asked us to pray. After calling all in the house, we held our hands together in a circle and prayed. She now strongly believes in the power of prayer. We also invited them to our Extravaganza, which will be in three weeks.

It was still raining as we were going to the car to drive to the Gonzales', our Mexican new members. It was a twenty-minute drive. I had called Maria Teresa, who told me that her husband was sick. Thus, I told her that I would try to visit with them today. It was still raining when we pulled into their driveway. After knocking at the door, we waited for a while. There was no response. Mary advised me to be patient. After a few minutes I knocked again. There was no sound. I knocked a third time. There was no response. The incident reminded me of two precious verses: "I slept, but my heart was awake. Hark! My beloved is knocking. Open to me, my sister, my love, my dove, my perfect one, for my head is wet with dew." Song of Solomon 5:2. And, "Behold, I stand at the door and knock, if any one hears my voice and opens the door, I will come in to him and eat with him he with me." Revelation 3:20. After this we wanted to visit Mary Kenyi, a Sudanese single mother, and Father Chris, a celibate priest who ministers with me, but the rain was pouring down heavily. So, we decided to visit our daughters. After being refreshed with a cup of tea we drove home. Surprisingly, we were not hungry, even though it was past 6:00 p.m. and we went without lunch. We remembered our Master's Word: "My food," said Jesus "is to do the will of him who sent me and to finish his work." John 4:34.

CHAPTER SIX

SHEPHERDING AND RECONCILIATION

9.11 2001 was one of the most painful days in American History. As it is with all our painful episodes, most of us remember where we were and what we did on that day and week. In my case, I was Chaplain at WT University and Vicar at St George's Church. As my wife and I were watching the horrifying new in TV, we had a knock at the door. It was a Police Officer who informed us that a member of our church, who was the treasurer, was very sick at BSA hospital. I drove as fast as I could. arriving at the hospital, I was informed that he was clinically dead. I prayed for him that God may revive him and he came back to life. The Spirit led me to pray for another patient who was also declared dead, and he came back to life. This was the very first time that God used me in this way.

The following day, both students and the faculty gathered at the Pole with American flag and prayed and sung Christian songs. It was raining but we neither cared about rain, or Marine O'Hare with her Supreme Court who ruled that it was against the law to have anything religious in public institutions. This day, we boldly claim our religious freedom. God filled us with boldness as he did to Peter and John when they were commanded by the Jewish Supreme Court not to speak about Jesus. Peter responded: "Judge for yourself whether it is right in God's sight to obey you rather than God. For we cannot help speaking what we have seen and heard." Acts 4:19

The following week I was led by the Holy Spirit to organize a community forum with Muslims and Christian lecturers as panelists. The Muslim teacher informed us that what the terrorist did was not in keeping the religious ideal. The Christian faculty reminded us about Christian ideal. The forum brought a better understanding between Christian and Muslims.

Thus, the message which we learn from 9-11 is that we should love one another and preach the message of reconciliation. As the Bible puts it: "all this is from God who reconcile us to himself through Christ and gave us the ministry of reconciliation, that God was reconciling the whole world to himself in Christ, not counting men's sin against them. And he has committed to us the message of reconciliation." 2Corinthian 5:18-19

CHAPTER SEVEN

BISHOPS WITH GOAT HEAD

MEETING WITH BISHOP

May 15, 2003, was the day that Mary had to leave for Kenya for a two-month vacation. Four weeks before this date we were busy with preparations. We had to buy things to take to my mother, mother-in-law, sisters, brothers, nephews, and nieces. These necessities, the airline tickets, and money for incidentals left us without any cash flow. While our accounts were depleted Rehema, our daughter, was hit by an uninsured drunk driver. Her car was totally demolished. Praise God she had no broken bones. The police officers, who came to the accident scene, wondered how she was still alive. She had to go to the hospital for a medical checkup. She had no health insurance and lived on a tight budget. We had to assist her with the towing expenses. When it rains it pours. We were left with no cash.

A day before the departure Mary worked nonstop. She had to see to it that a lady would coordinate Sunday refreshments at St. Cyprian's when she was gone. She had also to see to it that Isaac and I had enough food for two months. I tried to discourage her from this work, but it was as if trying to force a fish not to swim. She had to be the best mother and wife in absentia. She went on and on until midnight.

On the day of departure, she woke at 7:00 a.m. and by 8:30 a.m. we were in Amarillo International Airport. We found Rehema, who worked at the airport, waiting at the ticket counter. Looking at her I perceivedsomething was wrong, but she didn't want her mom to know about it. While Mary was busy talking with her nephew Benson, Rehema whispered to me that Mary's tickets were not found in the computer. "But don't let mom know about this. I have talked to the manager and he is working on it." After 45 minutes the itinerary was computerized. Rehema also arranged that her mom be treated as a VIP and be assisted by someone with a cart in all the airports. All that she had to take care of was her passport and tickets. After her two suitcases were processed, we escorted her to the departure gate. We then gave her a goodbye hug and headed to Canyon. As we were driving, I reflected on how Mary had given all her heart, mind, and energy to the new church and her family.She didn't have enough time for herself.Yet the Lord was taking care of her. I remembered the word of the Apostle Peter: "Cast all your cares upon him, for he cares for you."

I had not informed Mary that I had an appointment with the bishop. Somehow, I was sensing disappointment. It was now six and a half months since the bishop visited with me.After meeting with the bishop's committee, he informed me then that he had decided to appoint me as a missioner to St. Cyprian's Church and I would start work in January 2003.I would continue to reside in the vicarage. He further told me that there were funds for six months.

I had, however, good news to share with the bishop. The church had been increasing in number. We had at least five new members every month. While we had existed for only thirteen months, we now had a Canterbury program for the students attending Amarillo College that included four Bible study groups: junior acolyte, senior acolyte, and two adult Bible study groups. One adult study group concentrated on Mexicans, while another concentrated-on Africans. We hold bimonthly Gospel Extravaganzas in which we celebrate our diversity by praising God with all languages represented, and then we enjoy international cuisines. This momentous event brings Muslims and Christians together. We also had a strong Sunday school program headed by Jo Snead of St. Peter's Episcopal Church. We had Sunday school teachers from St. Peter's and St. George's. They were all godly Anglo Americans.

The uniqueness of the congregation lays in the fact it is the most integrated and fastest growing in the diocese. It also is a wedge to the Muslims. African Muslims regard Mary and me as their spiritual leaders. They call us whenever they have crises. Some come to church for healing prayer. So' I have so many things to share with the bishop. I am meeting with him in his apartment at the Diocesan Conference Center. I knocked on the door and the bishop opened it. He appeared different. I made a comment about his beard and his weight loss. He told me that his host served him food with little or no meat and that he was feeling much better. He then offered me a glass of water.

After this I started sharing with him about the ministry. He appeared apprehensive. There was neither a word of appreciation or encouragement. After sharing the story, he told me that the reason for the appointment was to inform me that there would be no compensation for me after July, and that he is giving me this information as a brother so that I could adjust my budget. He would be able to provide $100 per service, which is the mount given to a retired supply priest. This meant reducing the compensation from $57,955 a year to $5,200 a year. He advised me to apply for a job elsewhere outside the diocese.

I was horrified to note that he did not show any interest in the ministry of St. Cyprian's Church. After his decree, I quoted a scripture that I was meditating on:

> "And I will lead the blind in the way they know not,
> In the path that they have not known I will guide them.

I will turn the darkness before them into light,

The rough place into level ground.

This I will do and I will not forsake them." Isaiah 42:16

After this the bishop closed our meeting with prayer.

The encounter with Bishop raised more questions than answers: Why does the bishop have nothing for me in the diocese? Has someone poisoned the well for me? Has someone put me on the street? Does the bishop really understand the model of my ministry? Why am I being penalized for implementing the Diocesan Mission Statement which reads: "The diocese will provide the energy, resources, and support necessary to help all our communities become mission outposts and where needed, to help plant new ones." Why abandon the newest mission while other missions that have existed for decades were still being supported? Are the Africans not a part of the Anglican Communion or of one holy Catholic Church? Are the members of St. Cyprian's excluded from "a great multitude that no man could number, from every nation, from all tribes and peoples and tongues?" Why do we recite in our liturgy?

"Let not the needy, O Lord, be forgotten

Nor the hope of the poor is taken away."

Why do we sing?

"In Christ there is no East or West
In him there is no South or North,
But one great fellowship of love
Throughout the whole wide earth."

Metaphorically, I felt like a hen that was being separated from her newly hatched chicks, or a soldier who is in the battlefield and receives information from the command in chief that his supply will be cut off. I indeed felt alone and lonely. The dream that included nudity was fulfilled. What shall I say? Why the priests? Are buffaloes not more collaborative than the priests? When hunted by a lion the buffalo's team together to defend the weak. They are determined to die in defense of the feeble. Why am I in the holy orders, which at a time is most unholy institution on the planet? Was it not religious leaders who plotted, arrested, and handed over Jesus of Nazareth to be crucified?

MEDITATION

Even though I was wounded, I couldn't start the day without meditation. After a long silence, the Holy be led me to the word of the prophet Isaiah:

> "You are my servant; I have chosen you and cannot cast you off.
>
> Fear not, for I am with you.
>
> Be not being dismayed for I am your God;
>
> I will strengthen you. I will help you.
>
> I will uphold you with my victorious right hand." Isaiah 41:10.

Powerful are these promises. The Great Provider is reminding me that he is the one who has called me, not the bishop. He has chosen me and he will give me unfailing support. The Omniscient is also revealing himself as the Faithful Witness and the Righteous Judge. He has a word for my accusers:

> "You shall seek those who contend with you,
>
> But you shall not find them; those who war against you,
>
> Shall be as nothing at all, For I, the Lord your God,

Hold your right hand. It is I, who say to you,
'Fear not, I will help you.' " Isaiah 41:12-13.

At this time the key words are: "You shall seek those who contend with you, but you shall not find them." I am remembering those who orchestrated my removal. I recall that the storm was triggered by an abundance of visions that the Lord had given me. The major vision was the establishment of a preschool program that would use the spacious vicarage, and would also allow the vicar/chaplain to purchase his own dwelling. I had researched and found that the average stay of a vicar/chaplain was four and half years. I learned that the primary reason for this is housing. I am one of the two priests who stayed the longest. The diocese had not taken steps to care for the chaplains through housing.

To my complete surprise, I was their cherished priest until I started purchasing a house. The Church was one of the fasted growing churches in the diocese. The idea of a black chaplain owning a dwelling ushered in the campaign of personal destruction and character assassination. I was also spending much time ministering to the poor new immigrant.

However, the word of God is powerful and not one iota of it will not be fulfilled. It was and is being fulfilled in my eyes. Those who contended with me are nowhere to be found, even though I still dwelt in the vicarage that was adjoined to their sanctuary. They indeed have no power over me. The guardian angel is protecting us day and night.

Nevertheless, I am still enraged. I am torn between the attitudes, "Lord forgives them for they know not what they are doing" and "When evil doers assail me, my adversaries and my foes, they shall stumble and fall." I am still too devastated to concentrate on "For I, your Lord, your God, hold your right hand, it is I who say to you, fear not, I will help you." I struggle to sing with the psalmist,

"The Lord is my light and my salvation, which shall, I fear? The Lord is the stronghold of my life, of whom shall I be afraid?" As powerful and affirmative as the words are, they are not answering the question: Why should evil, arrogant, and selfish people prosper while the righteous suffer? Why am I suffering for tireless dedication to mission Christi? Why did I bother to implement the diocesan vision statement, the vision of the National Church of 2020, which encouraged doubling the membership by the year 2020? Why was I so foolish as to not distinguish rhetoric from reality, the walk from the talk?

After being invaded by these endless questions I turned to the devotional books. I opened *The Stream in the Desert* by Mrs. Charles E Cowman. The theme is: "My expectation is from Him," Psalm 62:5. I am particularly enlightened by these words, "Every prayer of the Christian, made in faith, according to the will of God, for which God has promised, offered up in the name of Christ, and under the influence of the Holy Spirit, whether for temporal or for spiritual blessing, is or will be fully answered." These words are now like a sunbeam shining in the dark night of my soul. I remember that in the forty-five years that I had walked with God, there has never been a time or a minute that I approached him with faith that I did not experience his gracious presence. God is gracious, which is the very meaning of the name John. I was praying and owning the promise of "Fear not for I am with you." I am experiencing his sweet quality. He is indeed, with, by, and in me. His comfortable promises I now possess: "For I the Lord your God, hold your right hand, it is I who say to you, fear not, I will help you." The Lord has put a new song in my heart:

> The best book to read is the Bible.
> The best friend to have is Jesus.
> The Lord is my shepherd; I shall not be in want.

CHAPTER EIGHT

DEPARTURE FROM THE EPISCOPAL CHURCH

For seventeen years when I ministered with the Episcopal Church, I learned that three things were most valued: buildings, money, and numbers. All other things, evangelism, and pastoral ministry were secondary. The clergy of a parish having a magnificent church building and the most affluent members were greatly rewarded financially. Those who reached out to "one of the least of these my brethren" were devalued. I was becoming a liability by reaching out to the poor immigrants. Thus, the diocesan funds were to be saved from the clergy who were wasting time with a nonfinancial generating community. The following letter from the bishop that he wrote after our meeting underscores the point.

Dear John,

"I simply want to reiterate the details of our conversation at my apartment on May 15. As we spoke about then, the diocesan funding simply will not be able to provide the full stipend for you for the rest of this year, and I am not sure how much will be available in calendar year 2004, but I doubt seriously it will be a full funding of stipend.

As I said at that time, I believe we can assist the congregation with paying the $100 per service supply as you continue to serve them, and we will send that directly to the congregation and they can pay you out of their operating fund. During that visit I also told you that I will be willing to contact other bishops nearby should they have positions that might suit your gifts and abilities. I am in the process of writing that letter to those bishops now and hope that they will be in touch with you soon."

Even though we have had a fruitful ministry of the international and national communities at the university, His Grace was convinced that I could only minister to the Africans. It never dawned on him that Africans have diverse cultures. So, he wrote to his fellow bishop stating in part:

Dear D,

"I write to recommend to you the name of a priest who may well be valuable to you as you begin to reach out to 70,000 African immigrants now living in the Houston area of which I heard you speak recently. The Rev. John Githiga is a priest of the Diocese of Northwest Texas who originally comes from the Anglican Church of Kenya. In his younger days he began full time ministry as a catechist, later being ordained deacon and priest. John has been in ECUSA for 20 years, attaining a D.Min from Sewanee several years ago. He has been in a mission in Canyon and chaplain to West Texas A&M in Canyon for 7+ years. Last year he resigned to work with a group of newly arrived African immigrants in Amarillo. The diocese agreed to stretch to pay his salary for the first six months of 2003, but unfortunately, we do not have a resource to continue a full package for Father John.

Father Githiga can provide you with his full C.V. and any other information you may desire. I believe with a large number of immigrants in Houston area, he may well be able to build up the Episcopal Church in the area in a way that might take several years to do in NW Texas."

In this letter the bishop is falsely stating, "He resigned to work with a group of newly arrived Africans." I didn't resign. I was fired for planting a new congregation, in keeping to the diocesan mission statement and the prayers in Anglican Prayer Cycle. The vision of planting a church was not an either/or, but both and. The mission only added more ministries to Mary and me. We had three congregations: University Church, University, and St. Cyprian's Church. The campus parish included teaching New Testament studies, being president of the United Campus ministry, a yearly picnic of international students in our backyard, weekly student lunches and fellowship, and individual counseling. The University Church included weekly Sunday services, Wednesday services, and regular parochial ministries. St. Cyprian included the activities mentioned earlier. The ministry to the immigrants was in obedience to God's call of reaching out to the persecuted church. I did not intend to do it alone, but wanted to engage the people of God who included university students and the members of the University Church and other churches in the area. We were also obeying the Great Commission, "Go therefore and make disciples of all nations." All nations included Africans, Mexicans, African Americans, and Anglo Americans.

The grievous mistake that the bishop made was that he never consulted with the university community or St. Cyprian's congregation. The latter endeavored to visit with the bishop but he declined. For the seven years we ministered, God always provided the funding because it was His mission. We never had any problem of paying all our bills, including diocesan apportionment. There was a financial blessing in both the University Church and the diocese. But when the bishop resolved to withhold support from the voiceless, the diocese was negatively affected. The bishop's letter highlights this point.

Dear Friends in Christ,

"I am writing you about a matter of deep seriousness that is challenging our diocese. As I am sure you are aware, many members of St. Nicholas Episcopal Church in Midland have left both St. Nicholas and the Episcopal Church to form a congregation that aligned itself with a diocese in Uganda. St. Nicholas paid none of the apportionment for the first five months of 2005, a sum amounting to just under $50,000. Their total apportionment of $109,000 will not be paid in full. Those who chose to remain with St. Nicholas Episcopal Church do not have the resources to pay this sum. In addition; a $10,000 shortfall from other sources includes the now-defunct St. Cyprian's congregation in Amarillo. This has put the Diocese of Northwest Texas in a difficult financial condition. Not only are we in a cash "crunch" for the present, it appears that without help from individual members of the diocese, our situation will continue to deteriorate."

Ironically, by trying to save money from an "African" priest, the bishop lost two congregations to the African bishops and the financial situation in the diocese "continues to deteriorate." Led by the Holy Spirit and my conscience, I resolved to pull out from Episcopal Church USA and align with the Anglicans. As it was in the case of so many faithful and orthodox clergy who were called out of the Episcopal Church, I was served with a Letter of Inhibition. The notice of inhibition was sent to the presiding bishop, recorder of ordinations, secretary of the house of bishops, all the bishops of the Episcopal Church, and clergy and vestries of the diocese. The letter stated in part:

"This is to affirm the determination of the Standing Committee of the Episcopal Diocese decision, pursuant to the provisions of Title IV, Canon 10, Section 1 of the Constitution and Canons of the Episcopal Church in the United State of America, that John Githiga is inhibited from the right to exercise the gifts and spiritual authority as a Minister of God's Word and Sacraments conferred on him in ordination and is further inhibited from exercising any other priestly functions beginning January 26, 2005, for a period of six months."

THEOLOGICAL REFLECTION

At the personal level, this letter was not a surprise. I had been served with a directive that sounded like "If you take that route, you will see it." I had also visited with other faithful clergy who had received the same whip. I had visited with Father Chuck Filiatreau whose parish had transferred its canonical residence to the Anglican Diocese of Thika, Kenya. Chuck and Gretchen gave me a right hand of fellowship. As I was struggling to find where to go, Gretchen insisted, "I know where you can find a good bishop." "Where," I asked. "Thika," she responded. As I unconsciously repeated the same litany, Gretchen interjected, "I know who is a good bishop for you." "Who is he?" I queried, as though I didn't know whom she would recommend. "Gideon."

Gretchen was right. I knew Gideon as a brother and also as a clergyman who had gone through fire with his ungodly bishop for being a type A priest. Gideon also has a tripartite theological heritage, with a B.D. from St. Paul's United Theological College, Kenya, an STM from General Theological Seminary, US, and a PhD from Oxford University, UK. He is, of course, more educated than my inhibitor. And so, I took Gretchen seriously.

St. Cyprian's and I asked for canonical residence in Thika. By the time I was inhibited, I had moved from ECUSA. St. Cyprian's was one of five parishes in the United States under the oversight of Bishop Gideon, and one of hundreds of parishes in the United States and Canada under the oversight of African bishops.

By divine design, the Letter of Inhibition came to me while I was hosted by Father John and Mother Ruth Urban who had received the same notice. These godly ministers of the Gospel prayed with me and comforted me. They indeed had empathetic understanding. As we reflected on the unchristian practice of claiming power to take away the spiritual gifts of a servant of God, we learned that it drew from the feudal system during the Dark Ages, whereby if the landlord laid his hand on you, you became his property. So, they said church employed this inhumane and undemocratic system for the clergy who parted company with them. In my case, the system was not applicable, since I was not ordained by the bishop of the said Church. I was ordained by Langford Smith, bishop of Nakuru of the Church of the Province of Kenya. It can also be argued that had I been ordained by the bishop of the Episcopal Church, it is unscriptural for any human being to claim the authority of taking away spiritual gifts. Spiritual gifts are God given. As the word of God puts it: "There are varieties of gifts, but the same Spirit, and there are varieties of service, but the same Lord, and there are varieties of working, but it is the same God who inspires them all in everyone."

During the ordination, the community and the bishop authenticate something that is already there. The Kikuyu word for ordination is gukunura, meaning "to remove the lid and let it flow." In traditional religion it was believed that if God called someone to be a priest or a prophet, he had no choice. If he refused the ordination, he would suffer calamity after calamity until he removed the lid so that the prophetic gifts may flow.

According to the Biblical accounts of the calls, calling is God's business. It is something that is designed by God before birth. As the Lord said to Jeremiah: "Before I formed you in the womb I knew you, and before you were born, I consecrated you, I appointed you to be prophet to the nations." Jeremiah 1:5. It is God who calls, equips, and sends. And for that reason, there is no creature, not even the angel of light, with the power to take away the gifts that God has bestowed on us. Our gifts flow from the Being who transcends all that is seen (and unseen) and who has power over all that he has created. And thus, for another human being to attempt to take away the spiritual gifts, is very much like trying to pump water from the ocean to drain the ocean. Or as the Kikuyu say: "It is like grinding water with grinding stone." (Kuhura mai and ndiri). Attempting to take away spiritual gifts was like fighting fire with petrol.

It gave me increased energy and desire to reach out to all the people of God, people of all nations and all social strata. Our ministers included people like Father Chris, a white man, who ministered to the homeless. And because of that, though he was Anglo and Anglican, he could not qualify to minister with the Episcopal Church. Interestingly, most of the clergy who were inhibited by the said Church are mightily used by the Holy Spirit. They have brought many souls to the Kingdom of God. All glory to God. Amen.

CHAPTER NINE

PRESIDENT MARY AND THE GOOD SHEPHERD

This night Mary awake with laughter. "Why are you laughing?" I asked. "I heard people saying that I am the President." As you can see in the previous chapter, Mary always been dedicated in the ministry and she does not work for money. She spent 8 hours in the paying job and many hours in the ministry that God has called her to do. I panhandle, besides working in School and nursing home, she volunteered to minister to the sick and the dying through Hospice. She also worked a volunteer as a greeter at Texas Open air drama at Paro Doro. Canyon. She did pastoral visitation with me. She begged donuds where she was working refreshment for her children at St Cyprian. Her spiritual children believed that she had a donuds factory. But she begged to feed her children when we were fired; she was the one who suffered the most.

But more importantly, she takes care of her husband and the family. Her commitment to ministry started when she was a teen. At St John's Church, Nakuru, Kenya she was high in participation. She was the one who gave the tune to the chair and was Sunday school teacher. We both attended early Morning Prayer led by the pastor, and weekly youth program. She participated in the interdenominational monthly music extravaganza. She was the one who was to read a lesson in the family service. When she was 12 years of age, she read Isaiah 5:1-7. The Song of the Vineyard

I will sing a song for the one I love

A song about the vineyard:

My loved one had a vineyard on the fertile hillside.

He dug it up and cleared it of stones

And planted it it the choicest vine,

He builds a watch tower in it

And cut out a vine press as well,

Then look for a crop of good grapes,

But it yielded only bad fruit.

Here the 12 years old was predicting her ministry. As you can see in the previous pages, she is very high in participation. She is a fertile hillside and the choicest vine. She has drawn from many tribes and nations. Her pastors at St. John's Nakuru included Luya, Lou, Pokot, British, and Australians. She leaned confirmation class from a British pastor. So, in her ministry she doesn't see either the color and hear the accent. She sees children of God who deserve love and hospitality.

Owing to her dedication, she suffers the most during the firing of her husband. She also fights with her husband. In our first firing, I went with her to the office of the bishop. And when the bishop said that I have to go because of the accent and Africaness. Mary responded: "Bishop, let me ask you a question. ". Yes, Mary responded the bishop. "Are you a Christian?" "Yes." Responded the bishop. "If you are a Christian, be a shepherd to your priest. It can be cold up there." So as a president, she had the last word.

Being very Godly, Mary has always encouraged me to be a good shepherd to the people we minister with. She is a reconciler. Sometime I have been surprised by her advice as we part. At one occasion, her parting words were: "control your humor." Going to the WalMart the place where I send money to our global children.

There was a lady on the wheel chair in front of me. She asked a lady who was attending the customer: "Do you take jokes?" "No." responded the lady. She then turned to me and asked: "How about you?" "My wife has advised me to control my humor." I then remembered how we used to exchange jokes with the lady who was in charge. Her jokes became so belittling that I quit doing business there and moved to another store and was not found there for one year. When I returned, the lady treated me with lot of respect. Being the manager, she instructed other attendant to never joke with me. I also quit joking and this ended the problem. Mama Mary is a good shepherd to the people we serve. I also enjoy building her ego I like calling her many names which include Patrioca, Nyina wandu(the mother of the human being, Dr Mary Githiga esquire, Darling, Mwendwa(a Kikuyu word which means: "the object of my love. I consistently thank God for giving me a godly wife. Who encourage me to be godly?

The lesson here is that we have to build the ego of a baby girl. Mary's strong ego was built by her dad. He required that Mary see him first before he get out of the bedroom. She was his lurky bird. And he believed that when Mary visits with him, he will have a successful business day. You need to encourage the pastor and his wife. This way they will bear much fruits. I am most grateful to God who has given us pastoral care from our students and alumni. We also need to build up the ego of a boy child. My maternal grandmother started giving me self esteem when I was born, being the midwife to my mother, when I appeared, she reported to my father: "We have seen men and it is your father. And my mom continued building me up by calling me Papa (father). The seed they planted was nurtured by the community who gave my mother a nickname: "Wagatungu. Gatungu is the name of my maternal grandfather. Hence, Wagatungu means the father and the mother of Gatungu.

As my spiritual son Mabur Atak, told his congregation when we visited his church: Bishop John has so many titles." Interestingly most of my title means father. This include: Abuna(Arabic for father),Padre, Father John, Patriarch(Father of the nation), John 13, This mean we have Apostolic Succession and I am 13th Patriarch. All these titles originated from my grandmother. The lesson here is that when God give you a baby, give him or her name which will build up her ego. I am most grateful to my father-in-law who selected best baptism name for himself and his children. He is Hiram (who was a wealth man. And all his children were giving great Biblical names and Prince and Princesses. This included George (who was a King) Ann(who was a princess and the mother of Samuel, the Judge and the prophet), Jane(princess), These children became successful).

Thus, Dr Mary has a strong ego and being godly, has prophetic gift which revealed to her that her husband's humor plus strong ego can get out of control. She has also seen him being humiliated because of his humor. As this story highlights:

CHAPTER TEN

DO YOU SPEAK ENGLISH?

My wife and I were flying from Houston to Amarillo, Texas. Determined to finish up writing the story of the three eggs, I looked for a spacious seat in the aircraft. Mary was ahead of me. She found a row with an extra seat for me. But I spotted a row with three empty seats, three rows before Mary, at the emergency exit. "There is a seat for you here, darling." She called me three times, but I ignored her because I needed to update the story before we arrived in Amarillo. I knew Mary wanted to visit with me as we flew, but I decided to sit where there were three seats all to myself and I could work on my story. The flight attendant went through his regular chores and came to the emergency exit. Looking at him with a sense of humor, I asked, "But how do you open the door?"

"Can you read?" he asked. Before answering his question, he posed the second question. "Do you speak English?"

"Bokito" (which means "a little" in Spanish) was my reply.

He then shouted at me, "Move away from there!"

"I am just joking, I am a doctor," I responded.

"Even if you are the president, move away from there!" he shouted angrily. I then had to move quickly before he summoned the air marshal who could arrest me as a terrorist. I moved back to sit comfortably with my darling. Now the story of the three eggs had to wait until we arrived in Canyon

The most aggravating question for those in the diaspora is "Do you speak English?" I have had this question asked three times. The first time I was in Barbados. I had just finished leading the worship that included baptism and preaching. After the service I greeted the people of God. One lady asked me as we were shaking hands, "Dr. Githiga, do you speak English?" Some years later I shared the episode with a friend of mine who was British. Surprisingly, he told me that he was asked the same question in one of the same Island. His answer was "We manufactured the language."

The question has a profound meaning for anyone who is eager to give to and draw from all nations. The question is about intercultural experiences and intercultural communication. The question is basically expressing his universe of meaning. For him, the English language is the only one spoken in his parish. More often than not, New Yorkers and residents of other cosmopolitan cities may not ask this question. I have had the blessing of living in three university towns. I have never heard this question asked there.

Those people who have traveled in many countries know that there are as many versions of English as there are nations or tribes. The other continental language I speak is Swahili. I have also learned that each country has its own version of Swahili.

If you are called to minister in another country, you need to bear with the people of your missionary have different fashion of English. Also bear in mind that you will be misunderstood, know that a familiar word may mean something different to people of different cultures. A story is told of a young woman who was a missionary in Kenya. It took her a long time to gather a group of five girls. This lady opened her first meeting with a prayer and then concluded with "Amen." The word "amen" in the language of these girls meant "I am going to eat you." By the time the young lady opened her eyes, all the girls had fled for their safety.

Thus, as you try to reach out and communicate with people of different cultures, bear in mind that even the familiar words do not mean the same. For an American the word "dog" means a pet which is like a member of the family. For an African it may mean a watchman who should not be let in the house.

Intercultural communication requires that you listen hard, look at facial expressions, and delay your judgment. Do not try to understand it by the first phrase or sentence. Where you do not understand, ask, "What is that supposed to mean?" The more you listen, and the more you stay with people, who speak a different version, the more you will be attuned to their language.

When we started ministering to African Americans who had no college education in Sewanee, Tennessee, we had problems of communication. I bought a book on black lexicon to learn their language. It didn't help much. But we started the "each one teaches one" Bible study that met in their homes every week. Mary and I became attuned to black dialect. Within one year we had conquered the problem. The first few weeks they had a problem pronouncing my name. One lady took us to a black church and introduced me. "I know he is an African. I know he comes from Kenya. But I cannot figure out his name." The more we ministered with them, the more we loved them and the more they became a part of us. When we were leaving for Kenya, the leading lady asked, "Where shall we get another you?"

When I came back ten years later, I was surprised they remembered all my names and pronounced them well. So, we have to listen to the people who are different from us with patience and love. And eventually, the Spirit will facilitate the communication. And we will become good shepherds

Let us now get the meaning of "Even if you are the president, move!" There is a profound message for all travelers. As a traveler, you need to bear in mind that after 9/11 all travelers became suspects. Traveling in an airplane is not a joke. Flight attendants have a right to tease, but the passengers don't have this right. Thus, the best words that need to come from your mouth are "Yes, sir" or "Yes, ma'am." If you do not need what is being served, just say, "No, thank you."

However, realize that even with good manners, you are not free from humiliation. I shared the above episode with a passenger who sat with me. He said, "I had a worse experience than that. I work with an oil company and travel every week. On one occasion it so happened that the scanner at the security checkpoint detected the residue of gunpowder on my hands. I was searched and interrogated. Then they called my wife to find out whether my story and her story were the same." All this is done for the security of the passages. Nevertheless, this experience should not deter us from traveling. We should trust in God's protection. Pray before you start the journey. Trust in God. Trust his word, particularly Psalm 121 that concludes: "The Lord will keep you from all harm. He will watch over you. The Lord will watch over your coming and going now and forevermore." He will indeed bless the labor of your hands.

CHAPTER ELEVEN

THE GOOD SHEPHERD IN ZOE CHURCH

Last Sunday (9.19.2021) Mary and I attended Zoe Church shepherded by our alumni, Rev Eliaza Mundakikwa who graduated with Master of Divinity. The members are Banyamulenge from Congo DR. These children of God had gone through fire.

Many Banyamulenge came under threat from the rebel forces led by Kabila and others in the 1964 uprisings and sought protection from the Mobutu regime in Kinshasa, while others sided with the rebellion. The term Banyamulenge came to be used widely in Congo to refer to ethnic Tutsi Congolese in general from mid-1996. They became the target of ethnic cleansing. Rev Eliaza had a near death experience. He flees to the home of a faithful Christian from the killing tribe and when they learned where he was, they invaded the home demanding to know where Eliaza was. When his friend refused to tell them where he was, they killed him. So Eliaza still support the family of the man who gave his life for him.

Like Banyamulenge, my tribe, Kikuyu, were object of ethnic cleansing in 2007. So many Kikuyu were killed. They way the home was marked doors of the house by the killer 42-1. In Kenya there are 42 tribes. So, my ethnic group became minus one. If the killer succeeded in destroying a Kikuyu property, he was given $8.00 and if he killed the owner of the property, he was given $18.00. So many people from this tribe lost their properties. This was a good preparation of me to minister to and with Banyamulenge. Who are very spiritual and committed to God.

What we experience in the service is the presence of the Holy Spirit. They were singing loud, jumping and dancing in Spirit. There was a high degree of participation. This reminded me what the bibles say: "Where there is the Holy Spirit there is freedom" and the word of Jesus: "I have come that they may have life. And that they may have it more abundantly. Jesus said: I am a good shepherd, the good shepherd lays down his life for the sheep. John 10:10-11 the very meaning of the name of the church is abundant life.

After dancing and singing two pastors gave short message. Then Rev invited me to greet people and give a short message. I then ask Mary to come with me and sing our favorite song:

There is nothing too hard for thee dear Lord.

Nothing, nothing

There is nothing too hard for thee.

I then spoke briefly about our recent book THE FRUITFUL FAMILY. After which I handed the pulpit to Eleazer. He said how difficult it is to preach in the presence of his professor, who is also a great man in the world. He said: He is my father, and you are all his grandchildren. Eliaza message was from Joshua 1:6-9> he exhausted us to be stand firm and be courageous. After the message he asked me to pray and bless the people.

Mary and I were strengthened. And well nourished.

CHAPTER TWELVE

THE GOOD SHEPHERD AND VICTORY

My two brothers and I underwent through painful experiences from the bishops with goat head, whom analytical psychology terms as "his majesty the baby". The Anglican bishop in Kenya used transfers to punish the priest. Habel had these types of transfers. Gideon had similar experience three times. And, as you can see in *MINISTRY TO ALL NATIONS* and *FROM VICTORY TO VICTORY,* I was fired three times. The first one I was fired for my accent and africanness and writing the first edition of *CHRIST AND ROOTS*; the second one I was fired for being too ecumenical and the last one, as we have mentioned, for planting an African community Church for the Sudanese and other refugees and by having undesired member of the family living with us in the Vicarage.

Canon Habel's victory came after the retirement. With a fruitful family, he is financially secure and now he attends and minister to all denominations including Roman Catholic where he is occasionally allowed to preach. Gideon enjoys the same financial security and also has partner in mission with two European Dioceses and is a member of an international religious body known as FIVE TALENTS; which equips the church for economic development. He had a blessing of starting Micro finance program in his diocese and by the time he retired, the diocese had become a billionaire. I always enjoy the way he bides me fare well when I am returning to USA. "As you return to Canaan tell them you have come from Canaan."

When the Holy Trinity gave us the birthday present of All Nations Christian Church International on 7.27.2007, he graciously gave us rest from punitive firings. And gave us, unlimited freedom of service. The Holy Trinity has blessed us with spiritual children in every continent.

Thus, my beloved, if you are going through painful similar experiences, do not lose heart. Remember the loving Father is your shepherd. And, if the loving Father gave victory to three brothers, he will also give you victory. Remember, if you have suffered in Christ, you will also be glorified with him. As you continue fighting a good fight, remember that the Holy Trinity, who has all power and who foreknew what you would go through even before you were born, has provision for you.

If you are the bishop with goat head, who is motivated by jealousy to punish the servants of God. You need to repent and receive Christ as your Lord and Savior. Otherwise, you will be judged. Do not wait to hear the King of Kings say to you: "Depart from me you who are cursed into eternal fire prepared for the devil and his angels. For I was hungry and you give me nothing to eat, I was thirst and you gave me nothing to drink, I was a stranger and you did not invite me in, I needed cloth and you did not cloth me I was sick and in prison and you did not look after me." Matthew 2541-43.

CHAPTER THIRTEEN

POLITICAL LEADERS WITH GOAT HEAD

Being a child of two worlds, USA and Kenya I have witness pollical leaders with goat head and shepherd heart. Paul predicted this leadership and the people who elect them in 2 Timothy 5:3. "But mark this: There will be terrible time in the last day. People will be lovers of themselves, lovers of money, boastful, proud, abusive, disobedient to their parents, ungrateful, unholy, without love, unforgiving, slanderous, without self-control, brutal, not lovers of good, treacherous, rash, lovers of pleasure rather than lover of God. We have seen this quality of leadership. Trump is of cause in this category. I was horrified when I was in mission to Kenya, when my sister-in-law showed me a twit in her smart phone. It had come from the President of United State. It stated White are superior to Africans and Arabs. Being analytical psychologist, my quick feedback was: To get the best assessment, one has to give IQ test to every African nation (130,000) in their languages and then the Arabs in Arabic and then the whit to compare and contrast. This of Couse is what Paul had predicted- people will be love of themselves and boastful and proud. The Kikuyu have a proverb which state: "A proud person lies to himself that he is more handsome than anybody else. Being arrogant Trump refused to secede when Joe Biden was elected and Trump had to send "Proud Boys" to storm the capital on January 6, 2021. The date has a symbolic meaning. This was Epiphany when we celebrate the visitation of baby Jesus his go by the three kings from East. This was followed by Joseph,

Mary and the baby Jesus his go fleeing to Africa (Egypt) and the killing of innocent baby boys. If African was inferior, it could not be a home of refuse for the holy family. He left the country more divided. And he also lost his twitter account and was also removed from Face Book for be destructive messages.

One the other hand, we have had president with a shepherd heart. One of this is Abraham Lincoln. He was reconciliatory and laboratory. He fought for the liberation of African American and the unity of Northern and Southern states. And finally, he died for being a good shepherd. He was also so humble that one time he surprised his servant when he found Abraham shinning his own shoes.

President Baraka Obama had a shepherd heart. Not only that he left the country united but he also introduced affordable health care. I still remember a critical incident when I was ministering University Church. I visited a white parishioner who was very sick. I was perturbed when she told me that she cannot to the hospital because she had no insurance and that with the little money she had, she could not get insurance because she had cancer. So, President Obama solved these problems.

Politicians decide who get what and how much. In Kenya the politicians have given themselves big salaries and renumeration. Kenya is the side of Texas but with 47 counties each of which have a governor and MP. Kenyan is paid higher salary than American governors. To get this money they hiked taxes. Politicians are also grumbling public land. During the campaign they buy votes by giving money to persons with influence including bishops and pastor. Other politicians are giving money to youth money and alcohol to youth. The lock in due to covid-19 has even worse the situations. Poverty has resulted in marriage breakdown, violence in the families, teen pregnancies, suicide and killing in the families.

Leadership With Goat Head

There is a lesson that Political leaders in Kenya should learn from President of Tanzania, Dr John Pombe Magufuli. When he became president, the first thing he did was slicing the salary of the president and then of other politician and that money was used improve roads and economic development of Tanzania. Even during the covid-19 pandemic, he did not sell fear to his country and so he left the country in a better economic condition. And thus, in Tanzania there is less family problems because people has enough food,

Praise God, Presbyterian Church, Roman Catholic and Anglican Church of Kenya have refused to sell their churches as to the politicians. They have refused them to use churches as political platform. On Sunday the Archbishop of Kenya announces that not only that they will not allow churches to be used as political platform, but they have to work hard to reconcile the president with the vice president who has been fighting each other. It was discovered that the vice President, not only that he is throwing stone in the house in which he is, but has employed influence persons to campaign and curse president Uhuru. So, the Right Revered Ole Sabit is bringing reconciliation. He is a true prophet.

This faithful church leaders and following the foot step of the great prophets. It has to be stated that it is not easy to be a true prophet. I remember my professor at Vanderbilt University telling us: "if you are true prophet, you must be ready to be treated as one." Nevertheless, James tells us to count it a pure joy is we undergo through various trials." Mary and I having been rejoicing for what we went through for the bishops with goat head. While we felt pain when we were going through it, we also experience the Great Provider as a very help in time of trouble. We have learned that God knew what we had to undergo long before we were born. As we have stated, all the firing were followed by miracles. After our last firing and eviction from the Vicarage, God used three angels who provided us with enough money for down payment of our present home located at 70 Hunsley. Not that the Hunsley has seven letters. Symbolically, this means that we have to forgive seven times seventy. Amazingly two years after firing, we had seven properties, one two of which were apartment complex and one of them was duplex.

It has also to born in mind that God is not toothless grandmother. He is a power judge. Our last meeting with the Church committee with the bishop, their issue was that they wanted to rent the guestroom in the Vicarage. I still remind, Mary responding: "If this is they was for raising fund for the church, then let every member of this committee rent one of the rooms in his house." Of course, the issue was not our guest house, but they wanted to get rid of the undesirable member of the family who was living in the room. As I write this message it has been seventeen years since they evicted us, and they still don't know how to use the facility. The other day I passed their and found a note: "even if you have the key do not enter someone may be in." They also haven't got another Chaplain. As you can see in Bishop's letter, the diocese had financial problem.

The other Chaplaincy where I was fired for being too ecumenical. This was actually rationalization. Because you cannot minister in the University without being ecumenical. The issue was with the leader of the small congregation who I referred as Lay Pope. He was a master mason and he and his followed had trio ideal- money, power and sexual immorality. This was indeed against my ideal. He had also made priests who were before me and were spiritual fired. And he had instructed his family that if he dies, he would not like Father Githiga officiate his funeral. The battle with lay Pope became fierce after I had taken a mission to Kenya where equipped priest and their spouses and three High Schools each of which had no less than 800 students. The seven missioners were described as: "people with pure heart. These missioners returned being more transform, and one of them who were a retired Vice President of the University organized Prayer Breakfaster for the

University community which was attended by over 200 persons. Seeing this miracle, I was in the spiritual prayer language which included weeping.

After this the Lay Pose wages war with me. I still remember, coming from Diocesan convention. On my way I cried to God: "How long will you let this man sabotage your mission? It is not my mission oh God. It is your mission. Arriving home the very first telephone call came from the Lay Pope's wife informing me that the man was dead.

His funeral was officiated by the previous priest who had a very short homily which was directed to the Lay Pope. He calls him by name and said: "you have wrestled with powers- power in the University; power in the Church, you are now going to face the one who has all power." But what was a challenge to me was that the word went around that the man died for fighting with father Githiga. So, his small group regarded Chaplain Githiga as an angel of death. However soon after this I was called to another ministry in a different state.

The message here is that "there has no temptation has seized you except what is not common to man, but God is faithful, he will not let you be tempted beyond what you can bear. But when you are tempted, he will also provide away out so that you can stand up under it. 1Corithian 10:13.

CHAPTER FOURTEEN

KINGS WITH GOAT HEAD

The Bible gives the account of the kings with goat head who were motivated by jealousy covetousness and who refused to listen to the prophesied. Ahab for instance, wonted to possess the vineyard of Naboth. The latter replied: "the Lord forbids that I should give you the inheritance of my father." 1King 21:3. The king was angry and when he told his wife, Jezebel she planed the killing of Naboth Ahab decided to follow the advice of his wife rather than seeking God's will. Jezebel planned how Naboth will be killed. Elijah the prophet was sent to the king and delivered God's judgment: "In the same place that dog licked Naboth blood dog will leek up your blood." He also prophet the death of Jezebel. The king and his wife were killed as the prophet has prophesied. He died for taking the advice of his evil wife.

This story shows the danger of following the advised of an evil wife. There are Church leader who follow the advice of their wives without consulting the Holy Spirit. They eventually don't end well. But as we have stated, there is a price to be paid by the true prophets. As you have seen, God, who is a Great Provider and protector will restore what they have lost for being faithful to God.

The true prophet has also courage of challenging the false prophets. Elijah courageously challenges four hundred and fifty prophets of Baals. They have to prepare one bull and Elijah has to prepare one. And then they have to pray for the fire from heaven. They prayed for a long time and there was no answer, but when I Elijah prepares his, he asked them to poor water on it. When he prayed, the fire of the Lord fell and burnt up the sacrifice the wood, the stone and the soil and also licked up the water in the trench. When people saw this, they fell prostrate and cried: "the Lord- he is God! The Lord-he is God." There was a great revival. Elijah had four hundred and fifty prophets of Baal killed. After this Elijah prayed for rain and his prayer was answered. However, he felt alone and lonely. A voice is asking him: "What are you doing here, Elijah? Here what he says: "I have been zealous for the God Almighty. The Israelite have rejected your covenant, broken down your altar and put down your prophets with sword. I am only the one left, and now they are trying to kill me."I King 19:13-14.

I still remember the feeling I had immediately after my first firing. I felt alone. I happened to meet a Baptist pastor who has just been fired. And told me how he felt and what he asked: "where is everyone?" Like me he felt alone and lonely.

CHAPTER FIFTEEN

POLITICAL LEADERS WITH THE GOOD SHEPHERD

Queen Elizabeth 11 is a good model of the leadership with the heart of the good shepherd. She builds up her noble character when she was a girl. She did regular work and didn't fear to soil her hands. And eventually when she was a grown-up girl, she would change the wheel of her car. When she became queen she engage in philanthropy-she reach out out to the poor. God has rewarded her by being longest reining British monarch, the longest serving female head of state in history. Yet she has survived in spite of challenges and criticism. She faced republican sentient and critics of the royal family, particularly after the breakdown of her children's marriages and the death of her daughter- in-law Diana. Yet she continued reaching out to the needy. God has rewarded her with long, healthy and fruitful life. And today, at 95 years, she has a net worth of $425 million.

Abraham Lincoln was another Political leader with a Good Shepherd heart. He fought with all his heart for the unity of Northern and Southern States and the liberation of African Americans. And finally, who found him the ultimate prize. Like the Good Shepherd, our Lord Jesus Christ, he died for them. Abraham was so humble and at one time, he surprised his servant he found Lincoln brushing his own shoes.

J F Kennedy was another President. He fought for the humanization of the African American. Eventually, he became so famous that if we talk about JFK the American will know that you are talking about one of the greatest presidents.

The message, here is that we are called to liberate those who are dehumanized even if it mean paying the ultimate prize. We have to speak for the voiceless. When we are led by the Holy Spirit, we will participate in the ministry of the Good Shepherd who cares for all people. Being cultural anthropologist, I have learned that each people has something to over to the global village. I greatly cherish the unique culture of Panhandle, Texas which is characterized by gentleness and kindness. That if you are heading to a building, the person ahead of you will hold the door for you so that you may enter first. The other day I was coming from glossary store, Mary was in the car. As I was approaching the car, two white lady who were behind me said: "we will help you put everything in car." And so, they graciously put the glossary in the car. With great appreciation I said: "Thank you so much my angels."

The message here is that the major difference between the leaders with goat head, those with the heart of the Good Shepherd. Those with permanent goat head are led by Satan who is the enemy of God. They are thieves whose mission is to steal, Kill and destroy; those on right hand are led by the Good Shepherd, who came so that we may have life, and have it the full.

The message here is that when we are led by the good shepherd, to care for his people. There is a reward. As he stated: "The thief comes only to steal, kill and destroy, I have come that they may have life, and have it to the full." John10:10.Those with Good Shepherd is reconciliatory. As the Bible puts it: "All this is from God, who reconciles us to himself through Christ and have given us the ministry of reconciliation. 2Corinthians 5: 18-19.

CHAPTER SIXTEEN

A SHEPHERED AT THE EDGE OF A CLIFF

I had a dream in which I saw myself walking alone on a hilly road. As I was climbing, I got exhausted and laid down because of weariness. I was frightened to see the edge of a steep cliff at my right hand. As I was lying just a few inches from the cliff, I was petrified when I saw a sixteen-wheeler truck coming toward me. I had a dilemma. I had to choose between moving to my right side and falling into the abyss, or remain lying where I was and be run over. I opted to remain lying down. I thought the driver would see me and stop, but to my disappointment he didn't. Thus, I felt the truck running over me, and I was amazed that I was not hurt. I then woke up peacefully.

This dream was a graphic expression of my feelings toward the ministry among the Somali. I never had any dealings with them when I was in Kenya. Here in America, I had met a few of them, but had no connection. I heard many horror stories about them. That they are opportunists, liars, parasites, and shrewd. Two Somalis can work using one Social Security number. I have heard that they are all 100% Muslim and would never become Christian. As a matter of fact, I had never seen a Somali Christian.

I had already had disappointing experiences with the Sudanese. They asked me to help them start a church and I spent countless hours with them. I worked hard to get them scholarship aid. We got going-back-to-school materials for their children. I got them an English teacher. We gave them orientation to the American way of life. But when I fell sick with pneumonia and lost diocesan support, we were forsaken for greener pastures.

Now I am facing Somali Bantu. I had been reading about them. I knew that 210 families of Somali Bantu were expected to arrive in Amarillo. How did I connect with Somali Bantu? Accidentally. I was visiting a refugee neighborhood on South Austin when I met Abdi's family. They had just come from Kakuma, Kenya. Abdi spoke Swahili. None of the members of the family spoke either Swahili or English, but we quickly connected with Abdi. The connecting threads were that we were both Bantu, spoke Swahili, and had Kenyan experience.

After visiting Abdi several times and bringing groceries to the family, he introduced me to two other families. My invitations to come to church with me were not successful. Instead of coming with me, he opted to babysit the children of three families so that two mothers could come with me to church. That day I had four Kenyans and two Somalis in the van. The Somali ladies were wearing headscarves and long dresses. They looked like typical Somalis. One of them spoke Swahili; the other one didn't speak English or Swahili. We started with supper and then praise music, followed by Bible study. When I took them home, all the children were waiting for them outside. They were jubilant to see their mothers back home.

I started visiting the Somali Bantu more regularly. I took their youth, together with the Sudanese and Congolese, to the youth program that included games, food, and Bible lessons. Unlike other Africans, the Somali youth were insulting. One of the kids told me in Swahili as we were approaching the church, "Mzee, wajua kwetu ni dhambi kuingia kanisani?" (Old man, do you know that it is a sin for us to enter the church?) When I was driving them back after feeding them, the young man complained about the van. "I never enter a vehicle without music."

Despite their negative attitude, I decided to concentrate on one family, Mama Mnose and her grandchild Husain. I prayed with them and took Husain, who was sixteen, to church. I gave him an English-Swahili New Testament. I read the Bible with him, and he also read alone. But for him to accept Christ was, as it were, a matter of life and death.

Nevertheless, the dream, as with visions and prophecy, had an immediate message for me, the worldwide church, and countries like the United States and Kenya, both of which received Somalis. It is estimated that more than fifteen thousand Somali have migrated to America and European countries. There are a large number of Somali in Kenya. They all have one thing in common: They don't integrate with the society. The message for the church is that we must study the history and the culture of the Somali. We have to find out why they don't easily accept the Gospel and why they don't assimilate.

After studying the history of Somaliland, I learned that there was a small number of Christians in Somalia. Ironically, most of the Christians came from the Bantu, which is a minority ethnic group evangelized by evangelicals and the Wesleyan Church of the Nazarene. There is one Roman Catholic diocese for the whole country, the Diocese of Mogadishu, which at one time was estimated to have 100 members. During the early colonial era, there were virtually no Christians in Somalia. And even those who later became Christians were orphans from church schools and orphanages.

When the civil war started, the missionaries left without raising educated pastors. Eventually the Islamic militia confiscated all Christian schools and churches. Not only that, there were no church buildings and no legal protection for Christians. The jihadists label Christians "Ethiopian intelligence." And for that reason, they killed all Christians in Somalia. Mnasuur Mohammed, a Somali Christian, was beheaded by Sunni Muslims while they were reciting the Koran. Western and African missionaries who sacrificed themselves to feed the hungry were murdered. In November 2003, a Kenyan Christian working for Seventh Day Adventist Mission in Gedo, South West Somalia, was murdered by Islamist radicals. The attack appeared to be deliberately anti-Christian and anti-Western. In the same year, a British couple, working for SOS Children's Villages in Somaliland were shot dead by gunmen in their home inside the school compound while watching television. Worse still, they hunted Somali Christians in neighboring countries such as Kenya and Ethiopia. A story is told of a Somali Christian living in Kenya, who was tranquilized and taken to Wilson Airport (a small private airport) and flown to Somalia where he was murdered.

Thus, in Somalia, Christians are regarded as apostates from Islam who should be killed. In February 2003 a radical Somali Islamist group, Kulanka Culimada based in Mogadishu, issued a press release in which they called for all Somali Christians to be treated as apostates from Islam and killed.

It suffices to show why, in the dream, I saw myself lying helpless between a sixteen-wheeler truck and the abyss. The dream had a message for me personally, for the worldwide church, and for the global village. The message for me was that I could not reach the Somalis single handedly. It is not a ministry for a lone ranger Christian. It is a ministry that calls for the corroboration of many Christians. These should be a team of people who are funded and who have to study the history and culture of the Somalis and other Islamic countries. The wealthy churches need to fund these teams that are at the cutting edge.

It is reported that in Kenya there is a Samaritan group that is reaching out to Somali Christians. These and other ministers who are preaching the good news in Islamic countries need the support of the worldwide church. The wealthy Arab countries are funding their brothers in building mosques, Islamic colleges, Islamic newspapers, and Islamic think tanks. Christians should do better in supporting their own missionaries. This is the message for the West, which is receiving Somalis as refugees. It should know the price they will have to pay. They need to love and befriend their children and youth. Since Somalis do not integrate with other children at school, they are bullied, and this makes them indignant against the host country. This is a challenge, too, for teachers who can hold a friendly discussion with Somali students. A story is told of a concerned teacher who held friendly discussions with Somali students. They discussed Al-Qaida and their training cells. The teacher was surprised when the students told her that they knew their websites. She asked them to show her the websites on the school computer, but since school computers filter those types of the sites, they could not get them. The teacher took them to a computer outside the school and the students showed her the websites.

If you are a Somali Christian or if you are a believer within a harsh Islamic environment, be assured that you are not alone. Greater is He who is in you than the one who is in the world. Being a patriarch of churches and ministries in more than seventy countries, I know the Christians who are being persecuted in North America, Europe, the Middle East, and Africa. You are suffering because you are with Good Shepherd. While the enemy comes to steal, kill and destroy, the Good Shepherd comes that we may have life, and has it to the full. John 10:10.Hence we have a word of encouragement for you. The most encouraging words come from the Book of Revelation, which was written by a suffering pastor to the suffering church. He refers to himself as John and says, "…your brother and companion in suffering for the kingdom with patient endurance that are ours in Jesus." The Risen Lord revealed seven great blessings. But we must perform seven acts:

1. *We must see the glory beyond the present suffering.* When Jesus was facing the cross, he prayed: "Father, the time has come. Glorify your Son, that your Son may be glorified." See yourself as conqueror. Our Master said: "In the world you will have trouble. But take heart! I have overcome the world" John 16:33. Moreover, Paul assures us: "In all these things we are more than conquerors through Him who loved us. For I am convinced that neither death nor life, neither angels nor demons, neither present nor future, nor any power, neither height nor depth, nor anything else in all creation, will be able to separate us from the love of God that is in Christ Jesus our Lord." Romans 8:37-39.
2. *We must bear the cross.* To bear the cross implies that we have to be faithful and obedient to God no matter the cost. We must suffer with Christ that we may be glorified with him. We suffer with Christ because we are God's children. I like the way St. Paul puts it: "The Spirit himself testifies with our spirits that we are God's children. Now if we are children, then we are heirs—heirs of God and co-heirs with Christ, if indeed we share in his sufferings in order that we may also share in His glory." Romans 8:16-17.
3. *We must rekindle the first love.* Remember how you used to have time for fellowship with God and the people of God? How you used to put God first in all things? The word of the Risen Lord for you is: "You have forsaken the first love. Remember the height from which you have fallen! Repent and do the things you did at first. If you do not repent, I will come to you and remove your lamp stand from its place. Revelation 2:4-5
4. *We have to be faithful till death.* Don't be scared of what you are about to suffer. God will be with you even in the valley of the shadow of death. He will clothe you with peace, which

passes all understanding. He did that to thousands of his faithful servants. He encouraged Bishop Polycarp when he was asked to deny the Lord's name. He courageously said to the killers, "Eighty and five years I have served Him, and he has done me no wrong. How can I deny my King who saved me?" The persecutor broke into the house of Andrew Kaguru, a lay reader who succeeded my Father. They demanded that he deny Christ. He courageously responded, "I cannot deny Christ. What you want to do, do it quickly." They chopped him to death, and he went to glory. There was nothing more they could do to him after that. He was far beyond their reach. Therefore, my dear brothers and sisters, "Stand firm. Let nothing move you. Always give yourselves fully to the work of the Lord, because you know that your labor in the Lord is not in vain. I Corinthians 15:58. If you are faithful only when there is sunshine, you cannot enjoy the victors' promise.

5. *We must not engage in sexual immorality.* No sodomites or fornicators will inherit the Kingdom of God. The Seer put it this way: "But the cowardly, the unbelieving, the vile, the murderer, the sexually immoral, those who practice magic arts, the idolaters and all liars- their place will be a fiery lake of burning sulfur. This will be the second death." Revelation 21:8.

6. *We must watch and prepare for Christ and keep God's commandments.* We must have oil in our lamps. We must "strengthen what remains and is about to die." We do this by reading the Bible every day and participating in Christian fellowship and worship. And by honoring God with our talents, time and treasure. We must live each day as though Christ is coming today. We must love God and man and all God's creation. Our Lord Jesus Christ gave the summary of the Law: "Thou shall love the Lord your God with all your heart, and with all your soul, and with your entire mind. This is the first great commandment. And the second is like

unto it. Thou shall love thy neighbor as yourself. On these two commandments hang all the Law and the Prophets." When we keep God's word, the Lord promised: "I will keep you from the hour of trial that is coming to the whole world to test those who live on earth."

7. *We must stop being lukewarm.* You may be like the church in Laodicea the seer wrote about. "I know your deeds, that you are neither cold nor hot. I wish you were either one or the other! So, because you are lukewarm—I am about to spit you out of my mouth." This is one of the dangers of materially wealthy churches. Laodicea was one of the wealthiest cities in Asia Minor. What do you get with material wealth? You need to commit yourself to prayer and immerse yourself in things spiritual and give generously for the mission. Heed the words of St. Paul: "Never be lacking in zeal, but keep your spiritual fervor, serving the Lord." Romans 12:11.

When you stay in the vine and practice piety and are the doer of the Word, all the promises to the seven churches belong to you. There is a precious affirmation in God's word. The Lord's promise is:

1. *You will be given the right to eat from the tree of life.* Unlike the Garden of Eden, fruit of the tree in the City of God is edible. The tree is on the bank of the river of water of life, which flows from the throne of God. It bears twelve fruits and its leaves are for the healing of nations. Right now, there are many Christians who are eating from the tree. If you are one of them, you know that you bear the fruits of the Holy Spirit, which are love, joy, peace, patience, kindness, goodness, faithfulness, gentleness, and self-control. You are also aware that you drink the living water every day. This being the case you enjoy the fulfillment of Christ's promise, "Whoever drinks the water I give him will never thirst. Indeed, the water I give him will become a spring of water

welling up to eternal life." This water can be illustrated with the testimony of a skinhead who committed himself to Christ during KAIRO prison ministry. His head was clean-shaven. His body was still covered with pornographic tattoos. He was two days old in Christ. He stood and said, "I have taken all kinds of drugs, which have put me high in different ways, but I have never been as high as I am this weekend. I had planned to kill some people after my release. But now, I plan to go and give them my testimony." Like the skinhead, when we eat of the tree of life, we attract people to Christ. They drink the living water and pass the same to others, and thus the water continues welling up into eternity.

2. *You will not be hurt by the second death."* Revelation 2:11. If you continue being in the True Vine and drink the living water, the first death will open an endless, joyous relationship with God. Jesus put it this way, "I am the resurrection and the life. He who believes in me will live, even though he dies, and whoever lives and believes in me will never die." John 11:25. Christ proved this promise by raising Lazarus from the dead. Better still, by being a victor; we will be given glorified bodies. For that reason, we don't fear death for "Death has been swallowed up in victory."

We can therefore ask with Paul, "Where is your victory? Where, O death is your sting? The sting of death is sin, and the power of sin is the law. But thanks be to God! He gives us victory through our Lord Jesus." I Corinthians 15:55-57.

3. *You will be given some of the hidden manna.* If we remain in the vine and continue to bear fruit of the Spirit, not only will we be unhurt by the second death, we will be given the hidden manna and "a white stone with a new name written on it, known only to him who receives it." Revelation 2:17. Those who have allowed the Spirit of God to fill every fiber of their being enjoy this blessing. They have inner contentment that cannot be put

in words. Paul refers to the gifts when he says, "Contentment and godliness *is* a great gain."

4. *You will be given authority over the nations."* Revelation 2:26. In All Nations Anglican Church we are foretasting this precious gift. I am awed by the authority that the Risen Lord has given the bishops who minister with us. They have the authority to invite my team and me to minister to their nations. I was thrilled by the authority vested in Bishop Stephen Vellaester by his community. During the medical mission, which took place in the dumpsite, the bishop brought together local medical doctors, military doctors, dentists, and student nurses from the local university who ministered to over six hundred patients. He even asked the military to give the poor boys haircuts. He ordered my team to provide medical facilities. And we all became brothers through service. The Lord has given us authority and power. Is this not what our Master means when he says: "All authority in heaven and earth has been given to me? Therefore, go and make disciples of all nations. And surely I am with you to the very end of the age?" Matthew 28:18-20.

5. *You will be dressed with white and your name will not be blotted out of the book of life.* This is another outstanding promise to the victors. They will be dressed in white. White is the liturgical color for Easter. They will enjoy eternal Easter. Thus, whatever you are going through for your testimony and obedience to God, be assured that you are among the great multitude in white robes. This is what John writes about them: "After this I looked and there before me was a great multitude that no one could count, from every nation, tribe, people and language, standing before the throne and in front of the Lamb. They were wearing white robes and were holding palm branches in their hands, and cried out in a loud voice:

Salvation belongs to our God,

Who sits on the throne?

And to the Lamb! Revelation 7:9-10

Not only will you worship God in white robes, our loving Savior promises, "For he who conquers I will never blot out his name from the book of life, but will acknowledge his name before my Father and his angels." Revelation 3:5.

6. *You will be made a pillar in the temple of God and you will never leave it.* After receiving authority over the nations (that is, you have an insatiable desire of giving and receiving from Christians of your own kind and those who are not your own kind) you will be made a pillar in the temple of God. You are one of the stones in the building. That is, you are a part of the Church Militant and Church Triumphant. We never give an excuse for not attending church. When you go to Church, you don't leave the church with dirt, but with particles of gold. If you are a layman, you are fully convinced that your presence is as important as is the priest's. Your attending the church doesn't depend on feeling, because you are a pillar of the temple of God. If you continue fighting the good faith of faith, you will enjoy what our Master has promised, "Him who overcomes, I will make him a pillar in the temple of my God. Never again will he leave it. I will write on him the name of my God and the name of the city of my God, the New Jerusalem, which is coming down out of heaven from my God, and I will also write on him my new name." Revelation 3:12.

7. *You will be given the right to sit on throne with Christ.* Revelation 3:23. "To him who overcomes I will give a right to sit with me on my throne, just as I overcame and sat down with my Father on His throne. Revelation 3:21. This promise has been realized by the saints who went before us. It is being realized today by those who are still fighting a good fight of faith, and it will be culminated when Christ returns at the end of time. The saying is sure: "If we suffer with Him; we shall also reign with Him."

Thus, whatever you are going through, realize that you are in the hands of Him who is and who was and who is to come. He is the Being who transcends time and space. Like the psalmist we sing:

I lift up my eyes to the hill
Where does my help come from?
My help comes from the Lord,
The maker of heaven and earth. Psalm 121:1.

Whatever you are going through, remember you belong to Christ and your life is hid by God in Christ. Listen to His comforting words: "My sheep listen to my voice; I know them and they know me. I give them eternal life, and they shall never perish, no one can snatch them out of my hand. My Father, who gave them to me, is greater than all; no one can snatch them out of my Father's hand." John 10:27-29. When you are at the valley of the shadow of death, shout to the enemy: "The Lord is my light and my salvation, which shall, I fear? The Lord is the stronghold of my life of whom shall I be afraid? When the evil men advance against me to devour my flesh, when the enemies and my foes attack me, they will stumble and fall." Psalm 27:1-2. Do realize that the enemy will use an economic crisis in the family to attack your soul? In the three incidents when we were laid off by ECUSA because of our faithfulness to the Gospel and obedience to God's will, funding was employed as a weapon. But our great surprise was that we never became homeless. We were never naked or without food. Thus, the more the enemy used that weapon, the more we realized that Ngai ni Ngai. That is, the Great Provider is the Great Provider. When the devil takes all your money, use Psalm 23 as your weapon: "The Lord is my shepherd; I shall not be in want. He makes me lie down on green pastures, he leads me beside the still waters, he restores my soul, and He guides me in the path of righteousness, for his name's sake. Even though I walk in the valley of the shadow of death, I will hear no evil, for you are with me, your rod and your staff, they comfort me." Even when you see the shadow of death, don't think that you are going to die. Be fully convinced that God is on the throne and that he has your interests at heart. God indeed watches over the preachers' wives who go through suffering with their husbands.

CHAPTER SEVENTEEN

EQUIPPING THE SHHEEPHERDS IN KENYA

On May 28 - June 25, 2010 the Lord gave us a clear vision as we set out for our mission to Kenya. We were to lead a retreat for pastors and to consecrate the shepherds of the flocks. The Lord assured us that He is our Great Shepherd and will provide for us, using us to empower the shepherds whom He had prepared before the creation to lead His sheep. The guiding scriptures came from Ezekiel 34:11-15. God promised: "I myself will search for my sheep and seek them out. I will feed them in good pastures." As with David, we were assured that "The Lord is my Shepherd." God also promised: "And I will rise up for I a faithful priest, who shall do according to what is in my heart and my mind, and I will build him a sure house, and he shall go in and out before my anointed forever." The Lord fulfilled these promises far beyond our expectations. All the events were like a divine carnival. We were fed spiritually even before delivering the message.

At Linana High School, we experienced God's mighty presence as 1200 young men were singing and dancing in the Lord. We were awed by the ministry of Chaplain Edward Etale, our seminary student. Rev. Mary and I gave the message to a very attentive audience. We sang for them "The Lord is My Shepherd" in Swahili. After the service we enjoyed hospitality from Chaplain Etale and then joined Bishop Ruth and Lisa Wong at the ordination of Martha Muzungu. This event was marked with joy. Martha and her congregation were very much like the name of their ministry, Joy Land Ministries. A delicious lunch included cutting ordination cake, which Rev. Martha fed the congregation as the bride would feed the bridegroom. I have never seen anything like it!

The retreat for pastors followed. The topics that were covered included fruitfulness in ministry, divine healing, and knowing your rights in Christ. There were praises and worship. The event concluded with a healing service conducted by Bishop Ruth and Archbishop Elias John. Most of the pastors were bi-vocational. The majority of them were teachers. Following the retreat, Bishop Ruth and I taught seminary students. Bishop Ruth lectured on Spiritual Formation, while I taught anthropological approaches to pastoral care. The students were eager and interactive.

The retreat was followed by the consecration of bishops George Mishandle and Stanly Karanja. George and his wife, Jenny oversees Four-Fold Church in Zambia; while Stanley and Margret oversee the Kingdom Builders Network that concentrates on reaching out to the teachers and the head students. We were very much impressed by the spirituality of these bishops and their wives. They are indeed a great gift to the church.

The next day we had the enthronement and consecration of the Archbishop Elias John Combo. The event was a musical festival! The service, which was held at the University of Nairobi, attracted a large crowd. Elias was consecrated as archbishop of the Vision Evangelic Ministries and All Nations Province of Equatorial Africa. He brought to All Nations gifts of healing. He preaches the Gospel with manifestations of signs and wonders, particularly in healing and deliverance. He has planted churches in all seven provinces of Kenya and has a ministry in Norway.

On Monday, Archbishop Kombo took the mission team to the Nairobi National Park. We enjoyed seeing all kinds of animals. The most impressive were a lion and lioness, who comfortably lay in the middle of the road as though they were posing for a camera. We drove closer and closer to them, but they refused to move from the road and expected us to drive on the roadside. As we watched them lying fearlessly, they reminded us of the Lion of Judah, and that with Jesus (the Lion of Judah) we can smile at the storm. They reminded me several times that I heard Jesus say, "It is I'd not be afraid."

On Tuesday, Archbishop Kombo took us to Masai Land. We were given a hero's welcome by the Masai who slaughtered a goat for us. Symbolically, this was an act of giving the very self. We enjoyed delicacies before the service. We were culturally and spiritually enriched by the Masai with their traditional clothing and African Christian folk songs. When preaching, we were affirmed by hand clapping. We left Masai Land rejoicing in the Lord who bonded us with the Masai. On the way to Nairobi, we had a flat tire in a small village. As we were working on the vehicle, two Kikuyu young men came and told us that they wanted to commit themselves to God. Mary and I delightfully led them to Christ.

On Wednesday, Archbishop Kombo took us to Ichichi, the place where I was born. The road was bumpy and hilly. We were totally surprised by the Holy Spirit in this church that is pastored by my nephew, Stephen Mbatia. We were given a warm welcome by the congregation that included my brother, sisters, and old friends. Bishop Ruth and Lisa were well received. There was heavy anointing and divine healing as Archbishop Kombo made an altar call. I have never seen this happen at Ichichi. To crown it all, the archbishop asked worshipers to come and shake my hand. Each person shook my hand and gave shillings that amounted to 750 Kenya shillings, which was a lot of money for an Ichichian. We felt loved, affirmed, and energized.

On Friday, June 11, we drove to Nakuru, Mary's birthplace. Saturday, we ministered to the Congregation of Yahweh, which is under the oversight of Pastor Susan, the wife of the Rev. John Mwaniki. We were once again awed by the Holy Spirit in the way the congregation (which was all Kikuyu, my community) worshiped in the Spirit and in Truth, and at the same time claimed our Jewish heritage. They preferred to address God as Yahweh and Jesus as Yoshua. Interestingly, there is a parallel between Jewish and Kikuyu heritages. For both, the fig tree is a national symbol. The meaning of the name Kikuyu is "the people of the fig tree." For both, circumcision is the means of becoming a full member of the community.

In the afternoon of the same day, we went to Kiti to minister with the Sudanese under the oversight of Archbishop John Thon. We were given a cordial welcome. The Lost Boys, who were clad in white shirts and black pants, performed Christian dances with a lot of skill and prepared the congregation for the message. Bishop Ruth had the message of encouragement for women, which was well received. After the service, we were served Sudanese traditional cuisine.

On Sunday, Bishop Ruth and I went to St. Nicholas Church, which I planted thirty-six years ago. This church birthed several parishes. It holds three services in English, Swahili, and Sudanese. The church is at St. Nicholas Children's Home, which I started 44 years ago. This church is my joy and my crown. We had arrived on Saturday to inform the vicar that we were in the city and would like to give a message. Before the service commenced, however, Bishop Ruth and I were called to the vestry and informed that we could not preach, but only greet people and sit in the congregation. We were invited to speak during the announcements.Ruth spoke for three minutes. When I stood, I spoke briefly for three minutes about how we started. During the fourth minute I was served with a note that said "time to stop."I then quickly remembered Paul's words: "Woe unto me if I do not preach the Gospel." So, I quickly told the innocent audience about the secret of a fruitful ministry, which is recorded in John 15:5. Our Master says, "I am the vine you are the branches. He who abides in me and me in him, he it is that bears much fruit, for apart from me you can do nothing." The incident also reminded me of the words of the Apostle John: "He came to that which was his own but his own did not receive him. Yet to all who received he, to them who believed in his name, he gave them right to became the children of God." John 1:11. We learned that the very meaning of being a bearer of Christ is rejection and reception.

After this Bishop Ruth and Lisa Wong departed for Nairobi while Mary and I were left visiting with families and friends. On the same day, we worshiped in Nakuru Cathedral where I was ordained a deacon and priest. Here we were well received and were given a chance to give a report about our ministry. We had a blessed meeting with the bishop of Nakuru and his wife, old friends, and members of our family. The whole service, which included a wedding, was uplifting.

Interestingly, although prevented from ministering at St. Nicholas, the following day, boys who had lived in the St. Nicholas Children's Home, found their way to a home where we were visiting. These lovely children of God are musicians who call themselves the "St. Nicholas Harmonies." They sang for us and expressed their appreciation. "We are most grateful you started St. Nicholas," said one of the boys. "If it were not for you, we couldn't be what we are." These fruitful children have produced a CD entitled "Jesus is the Answer." They eagerly listened to the story of how we started the home in 1966 and the church in 1974. They enjoyed immensely spending time with their "spiritual grandparents."

We spent our last week in Kenya visiting with families in Nakuru, Nairobi, and Ichichi. The word that the Lord gave us during our fellowship with the families was from Proverbs 17:17: "A friend loves at all times, and a brother is born for adversary." We praised our Heavenly Father for giving us brothers and sisters who are both friends and prayer partners. We also praised God for all our Christian friends who prayed for us and gave financial support to the ministry. The more you prayed for us and gave us financial support, the more the Lord used us as spearheads.

May God bless you and supply your needs according to His riches in glory.

CHAPTER EIGHTTEEN

CONSECRATION OF THE BISHOPS

Surprised by the Holy Spirit! This expresses what transpired at the consecration of Tom and Steve. The event was like a delightful carnival. Being a rite of passage, the occasion was preceded by challenges for Tom and Steve, as well as for Mary and me. When

we were being afflicted, we asked God: "How long, oh Lord?" This is a recurring question for members fof the faithful church on earth. There were also experiences that showed God's mercy. On March 5, we experienced untold traveling grace. As we were proceeding to the baggage claim at El Paso Airport, a lady gave us a ride on an electric cart the entire way there, where we found Tom, Sonia, Steve, and Mikah waiting for us. While we were being jubilant, Doyle and Bill arrived. Tom took us to the Marriot Hotel where we stayed for three days. Besides being in a wonderful facility we were given a fruit basket that expressed love from the Word of Life Church.

On the 6th we had a productive and beneficial retreat. We were surprised to note that besides having the same Spirit, the same faith, the same hope, and the same baptism, we had several connecting threads that made it possible for us to fly high like eagles. Steve and

I, although we come from different continents, had many things in common. We both invested in real estate and have the same number of properties. We were both students at London Bible College. Steve came from Aberdare in Wales; I came from Aberdare in Kenya. We both have written songs and published books. Tom has authored several books as well. Tom and I grew up with limited support and limited control, which made us adventurous. This is why although Tom was reared in the Church of God, he willingly accepted God's call to be consecrated in the Anglican tradition. Both Mary and Mikah experienced the challenge of having absentee fathers. Mary's father, a wealthy businessman, was exiled and tortured during the Mau Emergency. He lost all his properties and never recovered. When he came back from exile, he was depressed and died poor. This gave Mary empathetic understanding for the poor and the terminally ill. She has spent many years reaching out to refugees and giving care to the sick and the dying through hospice care. She does this without any salary. Mikah received God's call by seeing footprints that resembled those of her father. She responded to God's call by reaching out to male prostitutes, at her own expense, for four years. She won a good number of them to the Kingdom and a few of them became preachers. Like Doyle and Bill who grew up during the Great Depression, Mary and I grew up in a time of scarcity. In that era, discipline and hard work were the only ways out of poverty. In addition, four of us have ministered in the Cursillo and Kairos prison ministry (this is where we met Doyle). Drawing from these experiences, I am awed by the way God has given us the desire and will for working long hours. We praise him for answering our prayer, which is, "God, give me work till my life shall end. And life, till my work is done." We praise God for using the experiences from our families of origin to prepare us for fulfilling the Great Commission and the Great Promise: "Go therefore and make disciples of all nations." Matthew 28:19. "...You will receive power when the Holy Spirit comes on you; and you will be my witnesses...to the ends of the earth." Act 1:8.

Consecration, using modern services, commenced on March 7 at 7:00 with joyous and uplifting music. There was a heavy anointing of the Holy Spirit as we followed the liturgy. We really felt the love of God that the Holy Spirit had placed in our hearts. After the consecration the congregation applauded, showing great appreciation for the bishops-elect being entered into the College of Bishops. After a warm welcome, the newest bishops celebrated the Holy Eucharist. We were amazed to note that Tom had been using Anglican ways the same way we do at St. Cyprian's International Church. He used a single cup with the individual Christian dipping the bread in the cup.

As a theologian, I was delighted by the way the consecration of Tom engaged me in theological discourse. One critic who claimed to be an Anglican ecclesiastical authority called me with a question. "Why consecrate someone who is not an Anglican?" Before I could answer the question, the caller concluded, "You are not an Anglican bishop. Were you consecrated by your brother?" In a nutshell, the caller felt he was protecting Anglicanism from Tom and John. Is this possible? The study of the rise and fall of great empires reveals that each empire objectivized and left behind some heritage for the global village. From Sumerians and ancient Egypt, we acquired the art of writing, and from Greek empires we inherited democracy and the Greek language, which was used for writing the New Testament and is still used as technical terms in many fields. Religiously, we acquired the Eastern Orthodox Church. From the Roman Empire we inherited the art of government administration, road systems (which were useful in spreading the Gospel), and Catholicism. From the British Empire we inherited the English language and Anglicanism.

Once these heritages were objectified, they became available to all the people of God. Thus, neither these empires nor any individual has the capability of protecting their heritages. To protect Anglicanism from Tom and John is very much like trying to protect the English language from these individuals who already have English names and have written books in the English language. Besides, I have the blessing of being born to Anglican parents and educated in Anglican schools. I was a student in the Anglican theological institutions for seven years, and was an Anglican representative in an ecumenical theological college for five years. I was also ordained a deacon and priest by an Anglican bishop, and was consecrated as a bishop by an Anglican archbishop.

It has to be argued, however, that All Nations Christian Church International draws from three main streams of Christendom: Catholic, Orthodox, and Anglican. Our vestments draw from Roman Catholicism, the titles patriarch and archbishop metropolitan come from our Orthodox heritage and the Book of Common Prayer comes from the Anglican tradition. We focus on the Holy Spirit. Our vision statement is: "Empowered by the Holy Spirit, we preach the Gospel to all nations." By being in Christ, we bear the fruits of the Holy Spirit that are "love, joy, peace, forbearance, kindness, goodness, faithfulness, gentleness, and self-control. Against such things there is no law." Galatians 5:22-23. We bear the fruit of the Spirit by abiding in Christ who said, "I am the vine; you are the branches. If you remain in me and I in you, you will bear much fruit; apart from me you can do nothing." John 15:5. We are justified in Christ. "Therefore, there is now no condemnation for those who are in Christ Jesus, because through Christ Jesus the law of the Spirit of life set me free from the law of sin and death." Romans 8:1-2.

CHAPTER NINETEEN

WE GIVE WHAT WE HAVE RECEIVED

MISSION TO THE UNITED KINGDOM AND KENYA, June 3-July 3, 2014

What do you have that you didn't receive?
I have nothing that I didn't receive.

In June 3-July 3, 2014 we were in Mission to United Kingdom and Kenya. The more I reach out to all nations the more I realize that I only give what I have received. In retrospect, I realized that I have received much from many African communities. The East Africa Revival movement, which brought and nurtured me into the Christian faith, is comprised of all tribes in Kenya. My spiritual and professional parents include Hungarians, Dutchmen, Australians, the British, Canadians, and Americans. As the Bible emphatically states: "To him who received more, more is required." The intension of the mission journey to the United Kingdom and Kenya was to visit the people of God from whom I have received so much, including the Church in Kenya. I am most grateful to God who gave me the desire of my heart. The Holy Trinity also accorded me unspeakable traveling grace.

I boarded United Airlines in Houston on June 3, 2014, and landed at Heathrow airport on June 4, where I was cordially welcomed by the lady in uniform with the gracious words "Welcome, darling."

This set the tone to the hospitality and love I experienced in the Living Faith Diocese. Bishop Steve and Mama Mikah took great care of me. Ian our driver took us to places we had planned to visit. My desire was to visit headquarters and the people who have made enormous contributions to what I have and what I am. We visited the Boys Brigade Headquarters who helped us when we were starting the First Nakuru Company of Boys and Girls Brigade. That became the mother of all brigade movements in Kenya organized by Anglican, Presbyterian, and Methodist churches. Mary became the captain of the Girls Brigade (GB) and I was captain of the Boys Brigade (BB). The BB motto, which impacted our character, is "Sure and steadfast." The GB motto is "Seek and follow Christ." We spent quality time with Steven Dickenson, brigade secretary, and were overjoyed when Bishop Steve decided to start a BB and GB company in his diocese. This is a great program for youth and I would strongly recommend our churches to start this program. For more information visit www.brigade.org.uk.

In addition, we visited Oxfam headquarters, the body of Christ that helped me when I was reaching out to the troubled children and youth in Nakuru, Kenya. They assisted in putting up the first buildings of the St. Nicholas' children home.

The most rewarding time was a visit with Father Martin and Mama Cynthia Peppiett who are my spiritual parents and guardian angels. Martin was my vicar and mentor when I was a young evangelist at Nakuru. They ministered to me after I had nasal surgery. My beloved Africans could not leave me alone. The more I was visited and talked, the more I bled. African Christians stayed with me. They of course drew from African ontology: "I am because we are, and since I am, therefore we are." I don't know how Father Martin knew that I was just about to bleed to death. He came and took me to his guest house, where I stayed for two weeks until I was completely healed. If they had not given me a refuge you wouldn't be reading this message. When I was visiting with them, they gave me the number of Canon Captain Charles Dickens, who was my principal at Church Arm College, Nairobi. I was surprised to converse with him in Swahili. Better still, Father Martin gave me a biography of Bishop Neville Langford-Smith, who ordained me deacon and priest and was a celebrant at our wedding. After reading the biography, I had a great appreciation for Bishop Neville and the Church Missionary Society, which sent him to Kenya. Neville was the only European bishop in Kenya. From him I learned how to be "the only." During my ministry in the United States, I was the only African priest," which was both a blessing and a challenge.

The Ministry with Living Faith Church was awesome. This ministry was established by Bishop Steve Evans, whom we consecrated in Patriarch Cathedral in El Paso, Texas. The membership of the church includes fifteen nations. It is truly "All Nations!" They have maintained unity in diversity, which is a core value of Anglicanism. They worshiped in Spirit. They have a team of well-organized evangelists who preach the good news in streets and institutions.

On June 10, I boarded Brussels Airlines at Manchester with Dr Davis, and we were in Nairobi the following day. We were met by Archbishop-elect William who was chief organizer of our mission. He took us to Saba Saba, where we held the first clergy conference on June 12-13. The hundred clergy and spouses in attendance were very receptive with a give and take attitude. They gave Dr. Martin and me Kenya Gospels DVDs and handwoven handbags for Mary and Sara. On June 15, we ministered two churches at Ichichi, my birthplace. The liturgy in both churches was very spirited. They indeed worshipped in Spirit and truth. We felt the presence of God just as we had in the Living Faith Church.

On June 17, we journeyed to the Great Rift Valley. On June 18-20, we had a clergy/spouses' conference in Nakuru, Mary's birthplace, and where I was ordained a priest, ministered to the troubled children, and planted a church in the 1960s. The conference, which took place at All Nations Church, was coordinated by Rev. Gordon and Mary Onyango. Gordon was raised at St. Nicholas's Children Home, which we established with the aid from Oxfam. Our music team was St. Nicholas' Harmony, our children. They have been ranked as the best gospel team in the country. The conference was crowned by the ordination of Gordon and Mary. As at Saba Saba, the clergy were very receptive and hospitable. They gave me a Kikuyu Bible. Interestingly, I didn't have a Kikuyu Bible even though Kikuyu is my mother tongue.

On June 19, Bishop Thomas Gwako and his five-year-old, Joy, came for us at Nakuru and we drove to Kisii. The following two days we had two crusades in Kisii, and on both occasions the spirit was high and we were well received. At Ogembo twelve children committed themselves to Christ.

On the 23rd we left for Nakuru, but Father Martin and William left for Nairobi so that Martin might fly on the 24th. Canon Habel and I were in Nakuru visiting with families and friends, and ministering with Gordon and Mary. On Saturday, Gordon and Mary took me to the dumpsite where we started the ministry of troubled children in 1965. There we found pigs, birds, and people salvaging through the garbage, and small shelters for the homeless. Hilton Church, which was planted and is being ministered by Gordon and Mary, was in this neighborhood. On Sunday morning, we had the regular service with Mary leading the music while Gordon was leading the service. Both were wearing chasubles, which were graciously donated by Archdeacon Joe and Mama Marlene Cordero. We felt the presence of the Holy Spirit in the worship. In the afternoon, we had a marriage enrichment seminar, which was attended by Christians from several churches. We discussed the challenges that were facing marriage partners today and the secrets of success in marriage. There was a very high degree of participation. The event was crowned with a love offering for the patriarch, which amounted to 955 Kenya shillings. This was a generous contribution from the church at the dumpsite. May the Lord richly bless them?

To the end, we experienced amazing grace, love, hospitality, and the presence of the Holy Spirit, which is in keeping with the words of our Master, "God is Spirit, and his worshippers must worship him in spirit and in truth, for they are a kind of worshippers the Father seeks." John 4:23. As noted above I learned that I could only give that which I have received. Christians of many nations and tribes have planted seeds in me and thereby prepared me to minister to All Nations. I still remember the last sermon which I heard from Peppiatt in the 1960s: "By love serve one another." When I visited them this summer, he read this message: "I pray…that all of them may be one, Father, just as you and I are one, for you are in me and I in you. May they also be in us so that the world may believe that you sent me. I have given them the glory that you have given me that they may be one as we are one." John 17:21-23. This is indeed our prayer for all Christians of all nations.

CHAPTER TWENTY

A SHEPHERD DREAMED CARRING AN ELEPHANT

On November 29, 2014, I had a big dream. I saw myself carrying an elephant in what appeared to be an arena with spectators. I was amazed that I was not exhausted. I then woke and found that it was a dream.

Puzzled with the unusual dream, I asked my son Isaac, as we were driving to a Pizza Hut, if he would interpret the dream for me, and advise me on how I can ride on the elephant's back, rather than carry the elephant on my back. It so happened that he was attending a mandatory staff meeting, and having worked as a manager of a bigger restaurant, he knew the problem, but didn't want to be a know-it-all. So, he told me he was planning to behave like a monkey and for that reason "it is difficult for a monkey to interpret the dream." After this, I called my old friend Professor Francis Githieya, who comes from our ethnic group. He revealed to me that the dream had a message about my mission to India. He compared the Kenyan elephant to the Indian elephant. "Kenya elephants are bigger and untamed, so you cannot be on their backs. Indian elephants are smaller and tamed, so they will carry you." He also told me that hunters of tigers' ride elephants to safeguard them from the tigers. He reminded me of a Kikuyu proverb, "The elephant is capable of bearing its tusks." (Njogu ndiremagwo ni muguongo wayo). Also, in my community we have a saying, "Nothing is an elephant", when we are facing the most challenging undertaking. It is similar to the Biblical saying, "Nothing is impossible with God." This is what I sing most of the time:

There is nothing too hard for thee, dear Lord
There is nothing too hard for thee.
Nothing! Nothing!
There is nothing too hard for thee.

The image of the elephant captured the undertaking I was facing at that time, what I was planning to do, and what I had to face in the most challenging month of December. A day before the dream, my "to do" list included communicating with eighteen pastors and bishops around the globe about the position of education coordinator and with several accreditation bodies about the accreditation of our university, I was preparing two books for publication and was talking with three publishers. Being a tent maker as St. Paul was, I was negotiating with mortgage companies for a better interest rate for our rental properties, and planning the overseas mission for 2015, including missions to India and Kenya. Professor Francis' comparison of Kenyan elephants with Indian elephants was relevant to what I was facing, and the great expectations of the people preparing the missions. The Indian planner was more realistic. One of the planners in Kenya had so overpriced the cost of the Church Leadership Conference that I had resolved to discontinue dealing with him.

As it was with the Wise Men and Joseph who were warned by the Lord through dreams, the dream was warning me to get the elephant off my back. It was putting me into a receptive mode. I was prepared by three episodes. One came when I was in a grocery store and heard an Anglo uttering a Swahili word. I jokingly asked, "Did I hear someone speaking Swahili?"

"I just said mambo jambo," was the reply.
"Did you know the word 'jambo' is a Swahili word for 'Hi?'"

From there I decided to walk in Westgate Mall. After the walk I sat at the food court and ordered a glass of lemonade to sip as I read a book from Free Grace on the *Deity of Christ* that I am now receiving free from Free Grace. I was, indeed, riding an elephant. An Indian touched my hand and said, "Jambo."

"Jambo," I responded. I now had a second Pentecostal experience. After small talk with the Indian, I went on reading the *Deity of Christ*. I was being empowered! I was again interrupted by another Anglo with a question.

"Are you a pastor?"

"How did you know?" I queried.

"You look like a pastor."

"I am."

He said, "I am a Salvation Army pastor."

This was quite interesting since I didn't have either a clerical collar or a cross. I felt affirmed by God, as He affirmed Jesus, "This is my beloved Son, of whom I am well pleased." In the case of Jesus, after the affirmation he was led by the Spirit into the wilderness. The part I was interested in is, "And the Angels ministered unto Him." I prayed that the Spirit would lead Mary and me where we will be ministered to by angels. So, I called my nephew Isaac Methu in California and told him that we would like to be with them for a week. He graciously accepted and advised us to bring walking shoes.

Gracious Father accorded us inexpressible traveling grace. Through the security check, we were told that we didn't need to remove our jackets, shoes, or even belts. We didn't have to raise our hands to go through the scanner, a requirement that gave the terrorists a feeling of victory, for their intention is for all travelers, including senior citizens, be treated as suspects. As we were coming back through Ontario airport, the security officer sang ""Happy birthday to you" for Mary.

Five days with Methus' family was indeed a sabbatical rest. We stayed in a motel, where we did nothing but rest. We didn't even have to make the beds. Breakfast started at 6:00 a.m. and was served until 11:00 a.m. This allowed us to sleep late. With my nephews and their families, we walked in a mall, a modern time cosmic center where humanity is nourished by humans. Beyond our expectation, we had lunch in a rainforest, which was peopled with animals. We sat beside the elephant. The Way wanted to reinstate the vision of the elephant. We appeared so small in comparison to the biggest living land mammal the Lord had created. It reminded me of the words of St. Paul, "I can do all things through Christ who strengthens me." And our Lord's encouraging words, "With God, all things are possible."

Relaxing and sharing the meal with Methu's family was a sanctification of life. Included in the family was my cousin, Isaac's mother, who is ninety-three years old with a good memory. We shared the story of my grandfather's family. He had sixteen wives, my grandmother being the youngest. Remembering our large family was a celebration of life. The challenges which most of us faced and overcame assured us that God was with us then, is the one who is with us, and will be with us tomorrow. He is the one who was, who is, and who is to come.

On Sunday we worshiped in Kingdom Interdenominational Community Church, which had begun in Methu's home. Now it is a big church ministered by two pastors, both with doctorates in theology. The music was uplifting, the message encouraging. Mary and I were called to greet the congregation, and then sang for them in Swahili Psalm 23, which has been encouraging us for the past 46 years. We were overjoyed to meet Dr. Peter Mwiti and Esther. Dr. Mwiti was my student from St. Paul's University, and so dear to me for being a successful student and specializing in my field. After church we had lunch with Isaac's mother and sisters and their families. I was awed by the intermarriages in my cousin's family. So, we enjoyed the meal and fellowship with many nations. This fulfilled my joy as the father of many nations.

As we shared the meals and conversation with Methu's family, I was astonished to note that we had many related experiences, which included challenges and blessings that we faced when we were in courtship. Elizabeth, who comes from Taita, one of the smallest communities in Kenya, faced challenges for dating a Kikuyu, who comes from the largest community. She stood her ground and stuck to Isaac for better or for worse. In my case, I was challenged by my family for dating a city girl. Being a young, dedicated diocesan employee, the challenge came from my bishop. It was reported to my father in God that I was dating an immature girl (Mary was just turning 18) and my beloved bishop stepped in by stopping our plans for marriage and transferring me from Nakuru to Eldoret—a hundred miles away. As I later learned from his missionary colleague, he did it so that the love between Mary and me might grow cold. After this, my father in God, who was a missionary from Australia, took a three-month vacation and left behind thoughts of Mary and me. Being also a church army officer, I was visited by the general secretary, Captain John Ball, who warned me about the course I had taken. But the more hurdles we faced, the more we loved each other, and the more we remained faithful to God.

When the bishop returned from his vacation, the very first thing I did was to visit him and tell him that I still loved Mary. We had a good ending in that the bishop gave us his blessing and agreed to be the celebrant of our marriage. As we were discussing these episodes, we learned that God allowed these obstacles to be in our way to strengthen our marriage. Interestingly, when Mary and I were facing these challenges, I was strengthened by Elizabeth's father, Mshila, who I visited with a college mate, Benhard Mshila. He made the statement, "Human beings can delay, but have no power of preventing God's will from being done." He supported his argument with Israel's flight from Egypt.

Hence, if you are facing challenges, if you remain faithful to God, God's will be done. If you are planning to do great things for God, be assured that no one can prevent God's will from being done. If you are facing an elephant, know that God is the one who created the elephant. If God calls you for an overseas mission, obey Him and you will be surprised by what He will do through you. Fascinatingly, I was enlightened by the words in a cup that was presented to me several years ago by my great niece, Marga, who is Mshila's great-granddaughter:

TO ACCOMPLISH GREAT THINGS,
WE MUST NOT ONLY ACT,
BUT ALSO DREAM.
NOT ONLY PLAN,
BUT ALSO BELIEVE.

While we must believe that there is "nothing elephant" in the eyes of God, four things are necessary: dream, plan, believe, and act. Five things are also valid: vision, courage, creativity, self-confidence, and self-control. VISION is the ability to see what others do not. COURAGE is the ability to act despite fear. CREATIVITY is the ability to think outside the box. SELF-CONFIDENCE is the ability to withstand criticism. SELF-CONTROL is the ability to delay gratification.

A visit with Prof. Peter and Esther Mwiti was energizing. Esther had prepared a delicious meal. The spirit was high and we experienced the love of God. The most rewarding were the memories of our time together at St. Paul's University in the 1980s when Peter was my student. Peter is my joy and crown for following in my footsteps. He specialized in my field and has written books on counseling. He teaches in two theological institutions and counsels.

Sharing St. Paul's University memories was rewarding. To my great surprise, Esther informed us he still remembers the license plate of the teacher's car in detail, but cannot remember the details of her present car. Surprisingly, I have always asked, "How come I still remember I had a Ford Escort KIA, but cannot remember the name of our present two vehicles? Did the automobile driven by the teacher seem that much different from our current vehicles? I remember my car was used for medical emergencies. If a student got sick during the night, I was called to rush him to the hospital, and we might stay until 2:00 a.m. But at 8:00 a.m. I had to be in the class teaching. Our salaries were so minimal that we didn't have enough money to buy gas to drive to Nairobi. To portray the best image to the student, we had to drive to Limuru, which was 8 miles, leave our car there, and board the bus.

Why we cannot recall a few letters and numbers, I have no answer. After finding this a common experience, I made the effort to memorize the registration plates of our Subaru and Honda Accord, which at this writing I have not succeeded in doing. The answer to this question will come from my students. Suffice it to say, our fellowship together with the Mwitis was very energizing.

Staying with the Methus gave us a good rest. They gave us many presents, more than we ever expected. As Isaac was taking us from the motel to the airport, he squeezed more gifts into our bags. This really fulfilled our desire of receiving, rather than giving. By the time we arrived in Canyon, our batteries were fully recharged.

The following day, which was December 24, the loving Father advised us to continue enjoying the Sabbath rest. No carrying or wrestling with the elephant. On Christmas Eve, we attended a beautiful Christmas service led by the Rev. Deborah Huffman of First Christian Church in Canyon. These lovely Christians housed our university, and regard Mary and me as a part of their family. On Christmas Day, Mary, Isaac, and I enjoyed ourselves.

The big lesson here for bishops, archbishops, cardinals, patriarchs, and popes is: You don't have to be a major actor on Christmas and other high seasons of the Church. Remember that you are a sheep, and the Great Shepherd can nourish you through the people of God. Said differently, you don't have to always carry the elephant.

However, remember to share your dream with the people of God. I shared the dream of carrying an elephant with Seminary students and my church. During the evening of Christmas Day, I listened to a message on my cell phone. There was the voice of Marcos Shalala from Nubia Mountain. He was inviting me to a Nubian community Christmas celebration. I was sorry to have missed the event. When I later visited with Marcos, he told me that he was carrying an elephant. He had been working very hard to bring the Nubian in Amarillo together. On this Christmas Day he had succeeded, but it was like carrying an elephant. Twenty-five families attended: twenty-one were Muslims and three were Christians. This, indeed, was an elephant. He wanted his teacher to see him carrying an elephant.

God can employ the image of an elephant when he calls us for a great undertaking. This may include physical suffering. St. Paul was knocked down and for three days he could not see, eat, or drink. Isaiah wrote how God spoke to him, "For the Lord thus spoke to me with a strong hand upon me and warned me not to walk on the way of these people. Isaiah 8:11. He said, Go and say to these people:

Hear and hear, but do not understand;

See and see, but do not perceive,

Make the hearts of this people fat,

And their ears heavy, and shut their eyes

Lest they see with their eyes,

And hear with their ears

And understand with their hearts

And turn to be healed." Isaiah 6:9-10.

The Lord of Host calls us to face the elephant. Some calls are preceded by intensive suffering. KTN interviewed a lady pastor whose call came after an agonizing experience. Early on the morning of her wedding day, she was raped by three men who stabbed her and left her broken and dying. When the police came, they couldn't find a pulse, so she was taken to the city mortuary. There they heard her coughing and realized she was alive, and took her to the hospital. When she healed, she planned what she called her "second wedding." On the night of their wedding, they felt cold and brought charcoal fire to warm their bedroom. Tragically, she lost her bridegroom through carbon monoxide poisoning. Her third wedding was successful. The unspeakable suffering led her to ministry. She is a wounded healer.

If you are facing an elephant, you need to find out whether God is allowing difficulty to come your way to get your attention. Share what you are experiencing with your spiritual director or a prayer partner. When Samuel was called by God, he went to Eli. He thought Eli was calling him. When he was called the third time, Eli understood that it was God who was calling the boy, so he advised the boy to say, "Speak Lord, for thy servant hears." When God called the fourth time, Samuel responded as he was advised by Eli.

A spiritual director is very useful in our spiritual pilgrimage and ministry. He helps us to know when to say, "Speak Lord, for thy servant hears." The interpretation of a dream is important both in political and spiritual leadership. Joseph became the second man in Egypt by interpreting Pharaoh's dream. He helped the world to survive seven years of hunger by his ability to discern the meaning in a dream. Daniel became second in command in Nebuchadnezzar's kingdom by interpreting a dream. Professor Francis Githieya had the same insight, as you will see in the following pages.

My friend, the Venerable Dr. Martin Davis, who is the ANCCI international liaison, and a professor of systematic theology, was my companion. We had planned a mission to India but God, who is omniscient, revealed that our mission would be to Sri Lanka, where one of the tourist entertainments is to cross the river on the back of an elephant. We would also see elephants walking with people.

God foresaw that Martin and I would minister in a Bible Church in that country. The vision of carrying the elephant without being tired was predicting our experience in this lovely country on the coast of the Indian Ocean. Interestingly, Martin had seen an elephant in his dream. Martin was riding an elephant but "Nothing was going well," unlike my dream in which I was carrying an elephant. God was revealing to him the difficult choices that we had to make in Chennai, India, and Colombo, Sri Lanka. They were choices between greater evil and lesser evil.

The words that highlighted our mission to India are in Mark 1: 12-13. "At once the Spirit sent Him to the desert and He was in the desert for forty days, being tempted by Satan. He was with wild animals and angels attended Him."

Mark puts in a nutshell Jesus' experience in the wilderness, and what Martin and I went through during our mission. Interestingly, our mission coincided with the celebration of Lent, Jesus' forty days in the desert. Surprisingly, the layover and flying time from Dallas to Chennai was 40 hours, marked with an abundance of grace and maximum challenges. There were wild animals, angels, and Satan. However, there were more angels than demons. On boarding Air Canada in Dallas, a young lady who was to sit next to I volunteered to put my carry-on in the overhead bin for me. And when I was going through security in Toronto, an officer asked me whether I was coming from West Africa. "I came from the United States," I responded. Had I come from West Africa, I could not go through Canada. I felt kinship with brothers and sisters in West Africa who have been ostracized by the global village because of the deadly Ebola virus.

In Frankfort, Germany, I asked the agent for directions to the gate where I had to board Lufthansa Airline. With great honor and appreciation, she took me all the way to the gate. After being in the air for nearly twenty hours, we arrived in Chennai, India. Fighting jetlag, as we were going through customs, we saw a big signboard with the words, "VISA ON ARRIVAL." Contrarily, we were informed that we could get an entry visa to India only in Sri Lanka at the Colombo airport. We were then led to a transit lodge and locked in. The second problem occurred when we were not allowed to purchase our tickets to Colombo. The man who locked us in had to purchase the tickets for us. He asked for our passports and credit cards. As the Kikuyu proverb puts it, "When the bull is knocked down it has no power to resist being marked with a hot iron." So, we had to choose between the lesser evil of surrendering our passports and credit cards to a stranger or being lock in forever. We, along with another American researcher, complied. We endured three agonizing hours as we waited for the tickets, passports, and credit cards. Our fourth inmate, a flight attendant from Sri Lanka, told us what we SHOULD NOT HAVE DONE. "You shouldn't have given him your credit cards and passports. You should have asked him to use his telephone and purchased the tickets over the phone." I felt butterflies in my stomach, or as a Kikuyu would put it, "I had water in the stomach." After the three agonizing hours the officer appeared, like an angel. We stayed in the lodge and slept sitting up the whole night. At one point I got thirsty and the lady inmate gave me a quarter gallon of apple juice. She also gave us useful advice about the Sri Lankans, "Be very careful. Those people can rip you off."

At 2:45 pm we boarded Air India for Colombo. We were surprised we were given entry visas to Sri Lanka. We were told that we could not get an Indian visa at the airport. Since it was Friday evening, we could get it on Monday. So, we took a taxi to the Ramada Hotel, which was close to the Indian Embassy. To our great surprise, the door to ministry was opened through our housekeeper, Pradeep. When he saw our crosses, he showed us great respect and told us he belonged to two churches, a Catholic and a Bible Church. Pradeep knelt down whenever he visited us. He made our rooms twice a day, and gave us extra bottles of water. We asked him if he would introduce us to his pastor, who delightedly invited us to be guest preachers on Sunday. On Sunday, Pradeep first took us to his home. His wife, who appeared to be very godly, greeted us with great honor. His children greeted us by kneeling and touching our shoes. We were seeing the humility of Christ in these children. I taught them a chorus,

There is nothing too hard for Thee, dear Lord.

Nothing, nothing, there is nothing too hard for Thee.

As I have noted, I like singing this chorus whenever I am facing an elephant. I was also preparing these angels for the time they will face an elephant.

After the visit we went to the church where we were warmly welcomed by the pastor. The service started with praise and worship, followed by our sermons. After the sermons, we had to pray and lay hands on each of the ninety Christians. All the children kneeled and touched our shoes. We experienced amazing love. We realized this is where God wanted us to minister. Returning to the hotel, Pradeep came in the evening to ask if we had had dinner. We told him that we were planning to eat a chocolate bar. He said, "No, you need to eat something." He took us to McDonald's and bought hamburgers for us. We experienced the compassion and generosity of God through Pradeep, who had a limited income. We now enjoyed being on the back of the elephant.

On Monday we took a taxi to the Indian Embassy. The agent directed us to another location. There we were directed to another office for photos. And there we were informed that it would take seven days to get a visa. From another source we learned that seven days may turn into seven weeks. We quickly decided to return to the United States. We had to buy tickets that we had not budgeted for. So, on February 24, we boarded Sri Lankan Airlines to Dubai, then Air France to Paris and Atlanta, and then Delta Airline took us to Dallas. Martin and I parted in Dallas and finally I flew with Southwest Airlines to Amarillo.

Being a student and a researcher by passion, I did extensive research on the political system in India. I found that European and American church leaders who were attending Christian conferences were denied entry visas. In the same month, two Catholic Archbishops who were to attend a liturgy conference were denied visas. Catholic News reported, "As Church leaders protested a rising tide of anti-Christian sentiment, and Indian government added new fuel to the protests by denying visas to two Vatican officials who had been scheduled to address a conference on liturgy next week." Archbishop Arthur Roche, the secretary of the Congregation for Divine Worship, and Archbishop Portase Rugambwa, the president of the Pontifical Missions, quickly cancelled plans for a visit to India after learning that they would not be granted visas. A spokesman for the Indian Bishop's conference said their bishops would press government officials for an explanation." However, we learned that the Indian government doesn't owe you any explanation when it comes to denial and cancellation of visas. In our case, we were being killed with kindness. Sri Lanka was a dumpsite for unwanted Christian leaders.

We further learned that in India Christians are being persecuted by both extremist Hindus and Muslims. Acts of violence against Christians include arson, re-conversion of Christians to Hinduism by force, threats of physical violence, distribution of threatening literature, burning of Bibles, raping of nuns, murder of Christian priests, and the destruction of Christian schools, colleges, and cemeteries. This girl, for instance, was burned for being a Christian.

And thus, by being locked in transit detention and being dumped in Sri Lanka at our expense, we were getting a tiny dose of what the saints are going through. We praise God for counting us worthy to suffer with the Indian saints. I can now claim, "I am John, your brother and companion in suffering for the kingdom with patient endurance that is ours in Christ Jesus." The words, which I got from our brothers and sisters were very encouraging: "I can do all things through Christ who strengthens me." This includes being crucified with Him, so that we may rise with him. We were reassured by his victorious presence: "Fear not, for I have redeemed you. You are mine. When you go through the waters, I will be with you. When you walk through fire you will not be burned. For I am The Lord your God, the Holy One of Israel, your Savior." Isaiah 43:1-5. I like the way St. Paul writes about the effect of elephants in his life as he faithfully ministered for the Lord; "But we have this treasure in jars of clay to show that all-surpassing power is from God and not from us. We are hard pressed on every side, but not crushed, perplexed, but not in despair, persecuted, but not abandoned, struck down, but not destroyed." We always carry in our body the death of Jesus, so that the life of Jesus may also be revealed in our body." 2 Corinthians 4:7-10. We were convinced that whatever happened will not diminish God's love for one another. In the words of St. Paul, "I am convinced that neither death nor life, neither angels nor demons, neither the present nor the future, nor any powers, neither height nor depth, nor anything in all creation will be able to separate us from the Love of God which is ours in Christ Jesus."

And to all those who are persecuting Christians, I would warn you with the words of the third century African church father, Tertullian, "The more you persecute us the more we will spread, for the blood of martyrs is the seed of the Gospel."

To all who are going through tribulation because of their faith in Christ, remember what the Bible exhorts us: "If we die with Christ; we shall also be raised with him." This good news is for our loved ones and we who have died in Christ. The Bible tells us: "Brothers and sisters we do not want you to be ignorant about those who fall asleep or to be grieved like the lest of men, who have no hope. We believe that Jesus died and rose again and so we believe that God will bring with Jesus those who have fallen asleep in him. According to the Lord's own word, we who are still alive, who are left until the coming of the Lord, will certainly not precede those who have fallen asleep. For the Lord will come down from heaven, with a loud command, with the voice of the archangel and with the trumpet call of God. And the dead in Christ will rise first. After that we who are still alive and are left will be caught up together with them in the clouds to meet the Lord in the air." 1 Thessalonian 4:13-17.

CHAPTER TWENTY-ONE

SHEPERDING IN SUDAN

December 24, 2013, found me at the lowest ebb and I was crying with the psalmist: "Oh my soul why are you downcast?" I was constantly listening and reading news about the newest nation of Southern Sudan. Looking at my 2009 diary, I learned that on December 24, 2009, I was in Duk, Jonglei State, which was having crises. I remembered how in 2008 God revealed to me in a dream the challenges that we had to face. The dream also predicted the current crises.

In the dream I saw myself with one of our Anglo bishops. As we were following our guide, my fellow bishop became sick and I had to walk holding his hand. Our guide, who was tall, walked faster without looking behind. As we were climbing the hill, the guide disappeared on the other side of the hill. As we walked with the bishop who was so spirited, but with physical weakness, the road forked. We didn't know which path to take. When we were in Bor, I saw the landscape that I had seen in the dream. Our fifteen days in Southern Sudan were characterized by exaltation and humiliation, opportunities and crises. Our schedule included visiting with then Vice President Salva Kirr and the governor of Jonglei stat. We watched the enthronement of Archbishop John and two other bishops, conducted open air preaching, saw the consecration of St. Paul's cathedral, and attended a clergy conference.

We flew from Nairobi to Juba on December 19 on a Jet Link jumbo jet, and on the 20th, we ministered the church in Juba. We went without breakfast, hoping for breakfast in the church. The service was spirited and went from 11:00 a.m. to 4:00 p.m. After the ministry of the word, women brought water in a basin, pulled off our shoes and socks, and washed our feet and hands. It was a challenge for them to put the socks back on wet feet. But we felt greatly honored. At 5:00 p.m., hungry and exhausted, we were led to a restaurant for dinner. We were accompanied by seven men. Each of them placed an order, but little did we know that we had to pay for everybody.

On the 23rd we chartered a plane from Juba to Duk. While this sounds great, we had not budgeted to rent an aircraft. However, we had the joy of having the archbishop, his family, and the diocesan staff with us. Landing at Duk, we were given a hero's welcome. We were led to the convention by the musical band. We felt loved and appreciated. I asked Bishop Doyle to be the first preacher. When he stood, he said, "I am not accustomed to this heat." As soon as he said that, he suffered heat stroke. Here the road forked, since I didn't know whether to take care of the bishop or continue from where he had stopped. The challenge was even greater since there was no hospital, no telephone network, and the plane had left.

The bishop was escorted to a small hut where he was given first aid by a deacon and two ladies. They were wetting his head and fanning him with a handkerchief. On one hand I had to deliver the word to a large multitude, and on the other I was concerned about what was happening to my companion. After the service, I went to the hut and found that my brother had recovered, even though he was still weak. I was led to a tiny hut next to that of my friend. This was to be my lodging. It looked like a Masai hut. To enter one had to crawl. The door was not secured and anybody could enter. Inside, the hut was too hot for my friend and so he had to sleep outside. The deacon slept next to him to take care of him. I slept inside where I was visited by lizards and crickets.

We were guarded by fifty young men, who slept outside the cathedral compound that adjoined our huts. They were noisy, however, because everybody tried to outshout the other. It sounded like the voice of many waters. This continued until 2:00 a.m.

On the 24th we had an enthronement service for Archbishop John and two other bishops that was attended by 2000 congregants. On Christmas day we had an open-air service. Those in attendance included chiefs and the congressmen. Six parishioners spoke before we preached. They told us about their afflictions. Two of them narrated how an Episcopal bishop had them arrested because they had become Anglicans.

On the 26th we had a clergy conference. Just as I started talking, Archbishop John told me that they had a gift for me and I needed to go and see it. It was a horned bull. I was told to touch it and pose for a photo. "It is not going to hurt you," said John. "It is yours to take with you to the United States." I told them to slaughter the animal for the clergy.

Immediately after this great honor the road forked. Going back to the class, I found my companion, who could barely stand because of his physical weakness, sidetracked by the clergy. They asked for clerical shirts, and they needed them here and now. Our guide had informed them that we would provide them with clerical shirts. The bishop told them that we brought only our own shirts. I had to take them back to class. We tried to engage them by using the

Bible discussion method, but we learned that the majority of them couldn't read.

After the session we were visited by the women delegates, dressed as our mothers used to dress fifty years ago. Their leader started with a question. "What made you consider visiting this place?" "Why?" I asked.

"Because this is a place where after God created the world, He forgot all about this place," she replied. "Look at us. None of us has ever gone to school. Besides we travel a very long way to fetch water."

These mothers requested two things: a girls' school and a well. Eventually, I learned that Dinka women are the most valuable and least educated. To get a wife, a young man has to give between fifty to a hundred head of cattle.

On Sunday we had a service with 1500 in attendance. The service started at 7:30 a.m. We were astonished to see that everybody had to bring their own chair. I saw children bringing cans that they used as a seat. We experienced the presence of God. Archbishop John spoke on stewardship, while Bishop Doyle and I preached the Gospel.

After the service the road forked again. Our guide told me that he expected us to provide the bishops with return tickets. Our funds were now depleted, but I gave each of the bishops $20. One bishop said, "This is not enough. I borrowed money to come here and if I don't pay back the lender, I will be arrested." We were made to feel guilty for sins we had not committed.

The night before our departure for Bor I had a nightmare. I saw a tall man forcing himself into my unsecured hut. When I woke up, I found that it was not a dream. There was a tall man standing in the room. He said, "You must provide the bishops with the money for their return tickets and you also have to fuel the governor's vehicle."

Learning that this was my guide, I told him, "Don't talk to me about money again!" "You are my father," he responded. "And I must talk to you as a son." He then left, but I couldn't sleep again.

In the morning the lovely mothers prepared chicken for our last breakfast. When my companion smelled the aroma, he could not even taste it. We encouraged him to eat, but he couldn't. "I know John will buy me some fruits on the way." Thus, after fueling the governor's van we started our journey to Bor. On the way we saw hundreds of head of cattle. But there wasn't a grocery or restaurants. My companion became sicker. He was vomiting constantly, but he had an empty stomach. This was bad for type 1 diabetics who are supposed to have at least four small meals a day. We arrived in Bor at night. We were housed with an Anglican lady, but she didn't have any food. Hence, we headed to town. As we were passing through a homestead, a group of short people stopped us.

A short young woman started beating our vehicle with a large stake as she talked loudly and angrily. Our driver, who was much taller and stronger, got a hold of her and grabbed the stake and threw it away. He then jumped in the van, reversed, and took a different route. He turned off the light and we had to depend on the moonlight. Driving through the bush, I feared that we would have a flat tire or fall in a ditch. As we drove, I asked the driver what the short people were saying. "Get away!" he said. "You have come to grab our land." By the time we arrived in town we had a flat tire. We changed it and then looked for a restaurant. There was only one. My companion asked me to bring him ice cream and canned beans. However, the only food that was available was roasted beef (nyama choma). The smell of roasted beef was offensive to my companion and he could not put it in his mouth. I was now concerned since he had spent the whole day with an empty stomach. Now he had to sleep on an empty stomach.

Worse still, in the morning of our last day there was no breakfast. The water for our shower was a handful of water that the hostess poured into the palm of our hands. We then had to go to Bor to board the plane.

While we were purchasing the tickets to Juba, the agents found that the dollar notes were older than 2005. He then took the liberty of reducing a dollar to 60 cents. We were left with $125, of which a $100 bill was unacceptable either in Sudan or Kenya since it was a 1999 bill. We flew to Juba, which I renamed Juba-poverty for the experience we had to face. We arrived at 9:00 a.m., an hour before the departure of the jet Link jumbo jet. The agent at the ticket counter told us that she didn't see our tickets in her computer, and that she required $600 for our tickets to Nairobi. As we were negotiating, the plane left. We were now two bishops in the airport who were very hungry, impoverished, and exhausted. While we were praying for divine intervention, the airport manager called the agent and us to his office. Looking the agent in the eye he asked, "Do you want to tell me that these two men of God are lying? And that you are right and they are wrong?"

"It is not me; it is their agent. We don't find their tickets in our computer."

The confrontation was effective. The agent told us to follow her downtown to the jet Link office. We had to hire a taxi and follow her. We had only 200 Sudanese pounds and $125. The miracle occurred at the downtown office. We called our travel agent in Los Angeles, California, and she spoke to the jet Link agent and our problem was solved. However, being New Year's Eve, there were no flights on New Year's Day so we had to stay in Juba one more day. We asked our taxi driver to take us to the United Citizen Lodge where our guide was. As we arrived, we told him that we were short of funds. "You are men of God," he responded. "Just give me what you can." We gave him 100 Sudanese pounds. This was angelic.

We were delighted to see Archbishop John. I told him that he had to find us some money for an exit visa in Nairobi. The following day he gave us $50. The providers had become beggars. We were indeed married to Lady Poverty.

In the morning of New Year's Day, we walked to Matumish Hotel, which was owned by a Briton who is married to a Kenyan. It was a half a mile walk. I held the hand of my companion as we walked as he was too weak to walk alone. When we arrived there, we enjoyed air-conditioning and watched CNN. We ordered breakfast, but were doubtful we had enough money to pay for it. Graciously, 100 pounds was enough. We stayed there for three hours, enjoying an environment that was closer to our own.

We didn't have money for two days' stay in United Citizen. We asked our guide to take care of it. He was now drinking from his own cup.

On January 2, 2010, we were in Juba airport. We now had $50 for an exit visa in Nairobi. But little did we know that we had to pay $75 for the airport tax. Now the poor bishops learned to bargain. I told the officer that we had only $50. By another miracle, he said, "It is okay." We boarded the plane. I sat next to a Sudanese American who was heading to the United States. We visited and he became a friend. He was another angel. I told him I had a $100 bill that would not be accepted in Jomo Kenyatta International Airport for an exit visa and that if he had newer dollars, I would trade him my 1999 bill for $50. My new friend joyfully accepted the deal.

After landing we walked slowly to customs. My companion had to sit several times. After getting the exit visa for $50 (this was all the money we had) we headed to baggage claim. I was overwhelmed with joy when I saw the driver of Bishop Gideon, my brother. We had no money for taxis, but now we had an angel driving us to the bishop's home. Thus ended our ordeal. Bishop Doyle received money from Rev. Carolyn and I had some money in Kenya. So, we both said goodbye to Lady Poverty, hoping she will not seduce us again. We stayed with Bishop Gideon's family for three days and recuperated. Then on January 6, 2010, we flew to the United States and on the 7th at 7:30 am we arrived in Houston. I was overwhelmed with joy when I saw Carolyn. She was another angel. I handed Bishop Doyle over to her safe and sound.

We can say that in all the things we went through, God was in control and had our best interest at heart. By being in Sudan for sixteen days, we developed an empathic understanding not only for the Sudanese, but also for the people of God who had undergone such tribulation. Better still, the Lord strengthened the bond between Archbishop Doyle and me. For sixteen days, we had no mirror (something we take for granted) and so we were mirrors for each other. We, indeed, owned a great promise, "You shall receive power when the Holy Spirit has come upon you, and you shall be my witnesses…to the end of the age."

Our Master fulfilled his promise. "And surely I am with you always, to the end of the age."

SOUTHERN SUDAN TODAY

As I am writing this message there are terrible massacres in Bor and Jonglei state. It is estimated that 10,000 people are dead and 825,000 have fled to the neighboring state. As Mr. Wai, an eyewitness of the massacre put it, "When I saw the bodies, I broke into tears." He said, "I was devastated. I don't have words to describe it. I was asking 'Why, why, why are they being killed?'" The questions why and what needs to be done, need to be addressed. The major problem is political. The power struggle between Salva Kiir and Dr. Machar. The two are poisoning their ethnic groups against each other. Politics also deals with the issue "Who gets what and how much?" There is an inability to accommodate diversity. Each community has a different language and culture. When diversity is not appreciated, there is a "thou-it" relationship whereby each community perceives the other as an "it." The most important question is, "What must we do to get out of the crisis?" As Pope Francis recommended, "Everyone needs to be a peacemaker." Peacemaking means talking positively about the other person and the celebration of diversity.

Sudan needs a prophetic voice from Sudanese religious leaders. This prophet should be God's mouthpiece who is fighting for justice without favoring his community, is willing to challenge his own community, and if need be, is ready to die for all communities. When Kenya was struggling with authoritarianism whereby the ruling party was the parliament and judiciary, it was religious leaders who had prophetic messages that dismantled the system. The battle was won when one of the most outspoken bishops -Bishop Alexander Muge- was assassinated. His death dismantled authoritarianism and ushered in a multiparty system.

Finally, it can be argued that only the water which flows from the people's desert can survive the heat of their desert. Thus, the answer to the problems in Sudan will come from the Sudanese themselves.

Nevertheless, as Christians we are called to stand in the gap for those who are suffering. The Bible admonishes us to bear one another's burdens. I like the way Apostle John puts it: "I, John, your brother share with you in Jesus the suffering and kingdom and patient endurance that is ours in Jesus Christ." Revelation 1:9.

CHAPTER TWENTY-TWO

MISSION AND THE CROSS

In March 2013as Dr. Martin Davis and I were preparing for our mission to Kenya, I faced something that I had written about, but I don't like experiencing. Pain. A week before we took off, I had a toothache. The dentist found I had a crack in my tooth and recommended a root canal. Before I had opened my mouth for the orthodontist, I looked at him and said, "Don't do a root canal if it is not absolutely necessary. If it is a gum problem, just treat the gum!" Surprised at a patient who spoke with authority, he looked at his watch, stared at me, and then told me they were going to take X-rays to make sure I needed the treatment. After taking ten X-rays, he told me that the procedure must be done before I left for mission. After sitting for two hours with my mouth open, I felt as though a big stone was grafted in my jaw. The enemy was laughing at me. "We have zipped his mouth. He will not be able to talk." Yet the Spirit spoke to me using the words of St. Peter: "Casting all your cares upon Him, for he cares for you." To my surprise, by the time we landed at Jomo Kenyatta Airport in a British Air jumbo jet, I had no pain. Gabriel, our tour driver, took us to the ACK guest house. The following day we visited Margret, my sister-in-law, who fed us a delicious lunch.

After lunch we drove to Murang'a. It was delightful to meet Bishop James who led us to the Queen's Hotel where we stayed for two days. All the clergy who attended the conference were

Spirit filled, teachable, and loving. Dr. Martin spoke about the Holy Trinity for hours without notes. I spoke about having a fruitful ministry. At the end of the event, we had an evaluation and found the following: We had the right audience-church leaders who were teachable with uplifting music, hospitality, and had give-and-take attitudes. They recommended that the next time we needed to talk about Christology. After the conference Bishop William drove us to Ichichi and we spent a night in his home. The next day Canon Habel insisted that we stay in his home. "We need you to stay with us because no Mzungu has ever slept in our home since the foundation of the world." During a family get together, Martin was the focal point of attention and everybody wanted a photo with him. Ichichi Christians were hospitable. Not only did they feed us, but they also took a love offering for us that amounted to 4,600 Kenya shillings. This was the actual cost of our travel expenses from Nairobi to Ichichi.

On our journey to Nakuru we visited St. Paul's University, which was my academic home for eight years (three years as a student and five as faculty). At the gate there were three women guards who had to check our vehicle, and then we visited with Prof. GalGalo, the vice chancellor who took us around. We visited Dr. Esther Mombo, deputy vice chancellor, who was one of my students. She reminded me about the Githiga Foundation Fund, which my brother Gideon and I started to award books to the students who excelled in pastoral theology and missiology, the courses we taught when we were faculty. As we were touring St. Paul's we got a call from Ken Otieno informing us that the pastors were waiting for us. We shortened our tour and headed to Nakuru, the city of my youth and where I was ordained a priest and where Mary was born. As we exited to go to Section 58, we found Ken who guided us to the conference sight. The music and spirit were high. During the morning of this day, I had advised Martin that we dress casually, but put on the cross. I was, however, amazed to find that most of the participants were wearing three-piece suits. Like the shepherds in Murang'a, they were Spirit filled, teachable, and receptive, and with inspiring music. But unlike Murang'a, these pastors came from different church families and different communities. They also requested that we come back.

The following day we toured Nakuru Game Park where there were thousands of flamingoes. This lake has more flamingoes than any other lake in the world. All the game was well fed and enjoyed posing for a snapshot. From there we visited St. Nicholas' Children's Home, which I founded for juvenile delinquents in 1965. In those days I hunted for children of the dumpsters. They were called children of the dumpsters and whenever children in the neighborhood saw my motorcycle, they sang "mapipa, mapipa" (dumpster). I am so grateful to God because ANCCI is feeding children at the dumpsite in Nakuru and in Iligan City in the Philippines. Now the center has many children, a high school, and the church we planted in 1975. After the visit we went to see Mary's sister, Jane, who entertained us and gave us lunch. We had a great time with the in-laws.

The following day we had to leave for Kisii. As you can see in Dr. Davis's report, the road from Kericho to Kisii was extremely rough and dusty. I felt for Dr. Davis who sat on the front seat, and for whom children were singing Mzungu, Mzungu (white man) even when he was trying to take a nap. Through God's protection we arrived at Kisi safely and were taken to the Mash Park Hotel. The following day we journeyed to the conference site. As Fr. Martin wrote, "The road was dusty and hilly, so by the time we reached the audience our black suits were dark brown and our heads covered with dust." The first thing our host did was to dust off our clothes and our heads. Entering the church, we found Pastor James Sobora from Tanzania teaching. He appeared to be a good teacher. Then Fr. Martin and I taught until 6:00 p.m. on an empty stomach. By this time, I was feeling exhausted and dizzy. Worse still, we had to climb the mountain because we were too heavy for the car. Driving back to the hotel we had a second dosage of dust. Upon our arrival Bishop Thomas gave me a prescription, "Take a liter of hot water." I drank a liter (1/4 gallon) of hot water while Dr. Davis drank a bottle of cold soda. We then appeased our empty stomachs with a chocolate bar. This was dinner for hungry and exhausted doctors. For me, dust and heat result in pneumonia or an asthma attack. Miraculously, I didn't suffer from these conditions. I didn't even use my inhaler. I am grateful to the Great Physician and for answering the prayer, "protect them hali na mali."

The following day, we had to journey to Kisii Mountain. As usual the people of God were full of joy. Better still, Sophia Gwako had instructed the women to prepare lunch for us. On the third day we had Sunday service, which was well attended. A large number of worshippers could not get a seat in the church and so they worshipped outside. Everybody danced in spirit. They all seemed to enjoy God.

We also had the blessing of ordaining three church planters as bishops with apostolic succession. After the service we headed to St. Angela's Orphanage. Astonishingly, when the children saw Dr. Davis, they thought they were seeing a ghost and so they fled for their safety. The only child who had courage was Angela. She was the very first child to be admitted and the orphanage is named after her. We had a good visit with the teachers.

After this we went to the church, which is ministered by Pastor Francis Matoke. We had met Francis on Friday when he showed me the Letter of Affiliation that I had sent him a few days before I left the United States. He was a victim after the election of 2007. He was shot with an arrow and had a scar on his head. His testimony brought tears to my eyes. He said, "I praise God for what they did to me. Before this suffering I didn't know God. But the suffering brought me to Christ. I have forgiven them and I pray for their progress." Francis' church included nine orphans. After the service we had a meal and a lovely discussion in his house.

The Kisii ministry, though most challenging, was also most fruitful. The following day we went to Nairobi and spent the night in the home of Bishop William Githiga. As usual, Helen prepared a delicious meal for us. Her compliment was interesting. She said, "I love you and I appreciate you because the only thing that you could not eat is a piece of metal." Bishop William appreciated me because I was cool and Martin because he was receptive, patient, and diplomatic.

The following day, William took us to Jomo Kenyatta International Airport where we began a 32-hour journey. Arriving in Amarillo in the evening of the following day, the weather was the opposite of what we had in Kenya. In Kenya it was very hot, and here we had eight inches of snow. Mary was unable to drive into our driveway, so she called Garang, our seminary student, to come for me. He succeeded in driving me home, but as he was driving home, his car slid in a ditch. Being too tired to do anything, I told Garang to take our car and the following day we would get someone to pull his car out of the ditch. The following day I had to call AAA who brought a wrecker. As the wrecker was struggling to pull the car out, it slid into the ditch. The driver tried to pull himself out without success. A four-wheel drive truck came to our aid, but the wheels started spinning. Finally, he was pulled out by a caterpillar tractor. The struggle took three hours. This was the day that I was supposed to sleep for ten hours. Being so tired and disorientated, I went to bed and slept like a dead man. After eight hours of sleep, I saw a little creature walking in the room. "Where am I?" I asked. "You are in your bed," the creature responded. "And who are you?" "You have been away only for two weeks and you cannot remember your wife?" I was so sorry to note that it was my dear wife who I had not recognized.

Once again, I had to face something I had written about but I didn't like going through. And that is confusion and temporary disorientation, which we undergo during rites of passage. The challenges were tripled by sleeping in seven beds in seven different bedrooms in three different time zones, and ministering with Christians with a diversity of cultures, plus jetlag. For more information see *Initiation and Pastoral Psychology* in the chapter on Lostness.

We are most grateful for all those who prayed for us and those who gave us financial support. I still remember a prayer of one of our seminary students: "Mungu uwalinde hali na mali" [God protect them in all circumstances (hali) and all that they possess (mali)]. I recited this prayer every morning. And God indeed answered the prayer.

To this end, if God calls you for overseas mission, know that he is able to provide and protect. In the words of our Master: "And whatever you ask in my name, that I will do, that the Father may be glorified in the Son." John 14:13. He also promises: "I will be with you always, even to the end of the age." Matthew 28:2.

CHAPTER TWENTY-THREE

SHEPHERDING IN SPITE OF CRITICISMS

Ezekiel 2:1-7, Psalm 123, 2 Corinthians 12:2-10, Mark 6:1-6

What should we do when we face criticisms? We learn from Jesus that we must continue doing well and retain a positive attitude. When we see the glass half full, the glass will eventually be filled and overflow with blessings. When we see the glass half empty, eventually the water of vitality will evaporate and then the glass is totally dry. We become dry rivers. We become valleys of dry bones.

Instead of becoming vital antioxidants, we become toxic. We become religious leaders with goat head.

Let us learn from Our Lord and Savior Jesus Christ how he faced these arrogant religious leaders. Mark reports: that Jesus "went to his home town accompanied by his disciples. When the Sabbath came, he starts to teach in their synagogue, and many who heard him were amazed. "Where did this man get these things?" They asked. What this wisdom has been given to him, that he even does miracle! Isn't this the carpenter's son and they took offense at him? Jesus said to them: "only in his own home town among his relatives and his own house is a prophet without honor." And Jesus could not do many miracles there. Even thou Jesus had done great things elsewhere. He had healed the sick. He had turned water into wine.

He fed five thousand with the picnic lunch of a boy. He taught as no one else had ever taught.

LEARNING FROM THE STORY

1. Great achievement does not always result in compliments.

There will be some who will be jealous. Put differently, no great deed goes unpunished. There are people who will be offended by what you are, what you have become, and what you have achieved, particularly the religious snobs who are dry wells. But like our Master we must continue to move forward. We have to keep on doing well. We must focus on the goal. We have to say with a loud voice, Wacha waseme! Let them speak! We should never view ourselves through the lenses of our critics.

2. Let the criticisms encourage us to excavate our best selves.

Remember your past paradise. Remember an episode(s) when you did great things. When you were cornered but came out victoriously. This led you to a deep meditation, which resulted in supernatural empowerment. Use those past victories to motivate yourself to face the present challenge. The apostle Paul is reacting to critics by "excavating his authentic self. His opponents are referring to him as "a little bowlegged man." Paul is responding with words. "I don't care what you say." I know a man in Christ who thirteen years ago was caught up in the third heaven, whether in the body or out of the body, I do not know. God knows. But one thing I remember is that he heard things that cannot be told, which man may not utter." You may try to put this man down! But on behalf of this man, I boast. As with Paul, concentrate on God's strength and your strength. Make the right choice.

Keep a positive attitude. We are really our choices and our attitudes.

You may not have control over what people say, but you have control over your choices and attitudes. I fully agree with Billy Riggs that "I fully control the two most important ingredients of a successful and happy life: my attitude and my choices."

Our Master chose to continue doing good works. He marveled at their unbelief, but didn't quit doing what he was doing. But he had to move to another territory. Do not force yourself on the people who cannot receive what you have. Instead move to another territory and continue doing well.

3. The story tells us that he could do no mighty work there.

This tells us that it is those who refuse what you have to offer who are losers.

Jesus did not lose, his countrymen did. He came to his own home but his own people received him not, but as many as received him, he gave them power to be children of God. They abased Him; yet God has highly exalted Him and bestowed on Him the name that is above every name, that at the name of Jesus every knee should bow, in heaven and on earth and under the earth and every tongue shall confess that Jesus Christ is the Lord, to the glory of God the Father.

4. As you keep positive attitudes and make the right choices, lift up your eyes to God.

Whatever is troubling you, commit to God in prayer. When we turn to God, our challenges become steppingstones rather than obstacles. We then hear the Lord talking to us as he did to Paul: "My grace is sufficient for you, for my power is made perfect in weakness."

Since his power is perfected in our weakness, we thrive where we are planted, whether we speak English or Swahili or Spanish. This is particularly true because, as the Apostle John saw, we belong to "a great multitude that no one could count, from every nation, tribe, people and language standing before the throne and in front of the Lamb. They were wearing white robes and were holding palm branches in their hands. And they cried with a loud voice, 'Salvation belongs to our God, who sits on the throne, and to the Lamb.'"

CHAPTER TWENTY-FOUR

CHRIST AT THE CENTER

African American Couple who have been married for 40 years revealed their secret of success: "we put Jesus in the center. He is first in everything. Consequently, God has blessed us with our three children. One of our daughters is a counselor in the University, the other in a manager in the Mall and the other one is a Lawyer." The husband who is a Pastor added: We also minister God together. A white couple who have been married for 68 years contended that it was God and ministry which cemented their relationship: "We ministered together" the husband stated. "When there was a pastoral call, if I was not there, she filled in for me." God has rewarded us by calling our son to the ministry."

Another Anglo couple who is co-pastors and has been married for 35 years revealed their secret of success: "we put God first, we are second, our children and everybody else are third. Whenever we get a new home, we kneel down and dedicate it to God. We have ministered here and as missionaries in Brazil where we started a medical clinic center. We use our money for the ministry and have always had a Bible study in our home."
Kim and Christ have been successfully married for 45 years. What is the secret of their success? Kim puts it this way: "Sometimes in our marriage I was tempted to walk away but the Lord Jesus brought me back to my husband. I didn't know the Lord when we were being married; I came to know Him after marriage. When

Jesus became our silence guest, we became more serious with our marriage vows. Unfortunately for the younger generation, marriage vows are empty words. For us they are powerful and binding; the younger generation marries to try out and if it doesn't work or if it is going to get tough, they break up.

John who has been married to Stacy for 50 years confessed. 'I was not good when we married, but when I was 34 years old, I committed my heart to Christ. After conversion I became devoted in reading the Bible and ministering to the homeless. And so, it was Christ in us and the ministry that builds up our relationship and gave us successfully marriage.

Roy who is a widower was married to the same wife for 60 years. He asserted: "the secret of our success was that we were both Christian and Baptist. So, the Love of Christ kept us together. We were also nurtured by our church. I loved my wife till death. I was with her when she was dying. After she died, I felt her presence in the room, for a while. I believe God took her to a better place."

Pat and Joan have been in their second marriage for 24 years. They asserted that the secret for their second marriage is Christ "We both failed in our first marriage because we didn't have Christ. The second marriage is succeeding because we have put Christ in the center. We also knew each other since first grade. When we put Christ first, we succeed in marriage because "He is before all things, and in Him all things hold together." Colossians 1:17. In Christ, we don't just put up with each other, we enjoy each other.

CHAPTER TWENTY-FIVE

NURTURE YOUR BEST SELF

In addition to being in Christ we need to nurture our best self by developing **five virtues: 1.Vision-** which is ability to see what others do not see. **Courage-**The ability to act despise fear. **Creativity-** the ability to think outside the box. **Self-confidence-** The ability to withstand criticisms. **Self-control-** The ability to delay gratification.

How do the married couples get vision? In the case of Mary and I, we are given vision when we are reading the word of God and praying in Spirit. As Our loving Savior told the Samaritan woman: "God is the Spirit and his worshipers must worship him in Spirit and in truth. As Joel prophesied: "In the last days, God says, I will pour out my Spirit in all people, your sons and daughters will **prophesy**, your young men shall see **visions,** and your old men will dream **dreams**." Acts 2:17. This is all about visions. Prophecy in seeing a vision about God' will for his people and prediction of the future. The vision may come in a dream at night when we are sleeping or even during the day when we are awake.

My vision for Mary was a gradual process starting when she was 12-year-old when she read Isaiah 5:1-8 in the family service at St. John's church, Nakuru Kenya. We were also the only teen who attended early Morning Prayer which was held from Monday to Friday. We taught children service and attend church youth meeting and youth camp where we were taught about friendship between boys and girls. We met at the home of her God parents who lived in the church compound. She was giving her sick godfather hospice care. As noted above we started the first Nakuru Boys' and Girl's together where I was the captain and she was an Officer of Girls Brigade. I started being attracted too her because of her commitment to God and the ministry. She was also developing feeling for me. She shared with me how they played a game with other girls about the first name of a young man with a vision that if she has the same number of the letters in first name, that man is likely to be your future husband. So, John and Mary happened to have the same number. But she was also looking for the character and the commitment to God and Ministry. So eventually we were spiritually bonding and I had to propose her in the presence of her godmother. She did not say yes or no. But we started dates. Having trained by Church Army to never let a young woman come alone to your house, we never had date in my house which was located at church compound all our dates were held at the city park we strongly believed that the best gift we will give to each other at our wedding was our virginity.

It is said that God does not give a vision without provision, but there is always a problem between a vision and provision. So, after dating, I reported to the priest about our friendship. Being an evangelist who was sharing the same pulpit with the priest who was jealousy of me; when I reported to the priest, without giving me a single word of advice, he reported me to our missionary Bishop, that I was dating immature girl(Mary is small in size-5' 2" - but superior in character). When the Bishop got the information, he quickly transfers me a hundred mile away from Mary as I later learned from his missionary friends, he did this so that our love may grow cold. However, our love for each other did not grow cold.

Our big challenge was that the bishop went for four months leave to Australia and Mary and I were left hanging in the air. To my great surprise, Mary's family was very supportive. My 5 years old brother in low, George said: "If they have evicted Captain John, we are going to build him a house at our backyard." May father-in-law comforted me with word: "When someone is playing the game, the spectators will criticize him. So do not lose heart.

When the bishop returned, I visited him. To my greatest surprise, he consented. I then asked him to be our celebrant. He agreed. I ask him to give us the date of the celebration. To my utter surprise, he said: "Mary will give us the date." I then joyfully went and asked her the best date. She gave us the date which was December 7, 1958. The bishop consented to the date.

We were amazed by God's provision for dowry, and wedding reception and honey moon. When my team visited my inlays to bargain the dowry my first advocate was my mother-in-law she said: "before you decide how much you are going to ask. Remember that Mary and John will need food after the wedding." My father-in-law responded: "all what I need is a pair of shoes." Then my team asks them to give a consent note. I was given consent even before I had bought a pair of shoes to my father-in-law. When we were planning for wedding reception, the team made so economical that we spent Kenya shillings 270 which was my salary. The wedding cake was provided by a British missionary, the bridal driver was bishop's secretary who was a British. For our honey moon we were hosted by a Scottish Presbyterian missionary. He left us in his mansion with a cook who not only provided us with dinner, but also bed room coffee. We were given lot of gifts-money and utensils. And we started our live together with enough provision.

The message here is since God is On our side, we should not run way from challenges. As the Kikuyu proverb puts it: Blessing are beyond the obstacle."(Munyaka bere ya kahinga). Remember what Joseph went through after his dream-Being thrown to the ditch by his brothers and sold as a slave and thrown to prison by Potiphar's wife. So, you need to see challengers as stepping stone, not as obstacle. We need to say with David:

The Lord is my light and my salvation-

Whom shall, I fear?

The Lord is the stronghold of my life-

Of whom shall I be afraid?

When evil men advance against me

To devour my flesh,

When my enemies and my foe attack me,

They will stumble and fall. Psalm 27:1-2

We have to learn from David, who in spite of being attacked by the person who were dear to him, the Lord protected him. He was attacked by his father-in-law because of jealousy when he killed Goliath and worm sang for him: "Soul has killed his thousand, but David has killed ten thousand. But Saul ended up by being killed by his arm bearer. Absalom, his handsome son, planned to overturn his father's government, but finally, God restore him and Absalom died in the battle. And thus, the Lord who rescued him from his foes, he will also rescue you from the religious leaders with goat head. As the Good shepherd said these enemies are thieves who come "only to still kill and destroy; but I have come that they may have life and have it to the full." John 10:11. Jesus has also promised that all those the father has give him, nothing can snatch them from his hand, for the Father who has given them to him is stronger than all. I still remember that when I committed myself to Christ as a teenager, my friend told me that I will not stay saved for one year. But the Good Shepherd has kept me in him for 63 years. The other day I was visiting with my brother Canon Habel with whom we committed to Christ the same hour like John and James. We praised God for keeping us in In Christ and has given us long health life. He has also helped us to bear much fruits. We then concluded singing our favorite song:

There is nothing too hard for thee dear Lord
There is nothing too hard for you.
Nothing nothing.
There is nothing too hand for thee.

All things are possible to thee dear Lord,
All things are possible to thee,
All things all things are possible to Thee.

CHAPTER TWENTY-SIX

FIGHTING A GOOD FIGHT

In the preceding chapters I have shared my blessings and challenges in the ministry. The following pages are intended to shed some light on the faithful ministers and parishioners. It is my delight to encourage all those who are called to fight a good fight of faith. It is for those who believe that they are called to bear the cross and so as to wear the crown. It is for those who are intentionally waiting for the bridegroom with the oil in their lamps.

When you are going through fire, you need to realize you are not alone. The Apostle Paul put it this way: "No temptation has overtaken you except such as is common to man: but God is faithful, who will not allow you to be tempted beyond what you are able, but with temptation He will make away to escape, that you may be able to bear it." I Corinthians 10:13. Do realize that what you are going through, Someone else has gone through it At one occasion after losing the pulpit due to a prophetic message, I met a Methodist minister who was very much interested in knowing where I came from originally. I told him that I come from Kenya. "Where in Kenya?" he asked.

"In a village known as Ichichi," I responded.

"I have been there," he responded with great joy. But to my surprise I learned that he too had lost his pulpit for the prophetic message, but God has called him to a more fulfilling ministry.

So whatever you are going through for your faithfulness and obedience to God's will, there is someone else who has gone through it. Be assured that God will hold you in the palm of his hand. You will make it! And it will leave you a better person. As the Swahili proverb put it, Kilicho na mwanzo kina mwisho. Whatever has a beginning has an end.

THE PROPHET'S REWARD

My pastoral theology professor at Vanderbilt University made a great remark in this regard, "If you are a true prophet you must be ready to be treated as one." One of the greatest gifts of the prophet is a joyous relationship with God, a relationship that makes him a mouthpiece of God. They experience the love of God firsthand. They enjoy the peace of God that transcends all understanding. They delight in having the knowledge of the secret of God and seeing the events before they occur. They enjoy foretelling and forth telling the will of God. Yet both Old Testament and New Testament prophets suffered for their messages. They were afflicted by unregenerate religious and political leaders, particularly when they were told what they did not want to hear.

Jeremiah is one of the prophets who suffered terribly at the hands of his fellow priests and prophets, and the kings. During the reign of Jehoiakim, Jeremiah was commanded by the Lord to go to the temple and deliver God's message to the prophets and priests. He was ordered by God, "Do not diminish a word." When he prophesied as he was commanded, he was seized by the priests and the false prophets, saying, "You shall surely die!" They took him to the king to be put to death. But he was rescued through divine intervention. See Jeremiah 26.

If God has called you to be both a priest and a prophet, you experience great psychological pain when your fellow priests afflict you. When this happens, think of Jeremiah. You need to bear in mind that the enemy's objective is to remove you from the church. In this case, remember that the visible church comprises wheat and tares, sheep and goats, five wise virgins and five foolish virgins, children of darkness and children of the light. You need therefore to stay connected with the children of light. Immerse yourself in the Spirit. Follow the footsteps of great men of God like Jeremiah and St. Stephen. Draw heavily from the Universal Power. This is exactly what Stephen did. Luke tells us, "And Stephen was full of faith and power, did great wonders and signs among the people." The greatest wonder took place when he was being stoned for his testimony. Luke narrates: "But he [Stephen] being full of the Holy Spirit, gazed into heaven and saw the glory of God, And Jesus standing at the right hand of God. And said: 'I see heaven open and the Son of God standing at the right hand of God. As they were stoning him his last words were: Lord Jesus receives my spirit, Lord do not charge them with this sin.'" Acts 6:8-7:60.

So whatever you are going through, keep on gazing to heaven to the Lord of hosts. Know that you have a special relationship with a loving Father who is always in control and has your best interest at heart. Realize that you have a High Priest who is sitting at the right hand of God who went through what you are going through. Are you being afflicted by ecclesiastical authority or a lay pope? Remember your Lord went through it. Are you condemned to death in "Jerusalem?" This happened to Jesus. He once lamented, "O Jerusalem, Jerusalem, and the one who killed the prophets and stoned those who are sent to her! I wanted to gather your children together, as the hen gathers her chickens under her wings, but you were not willing! See! Your house is desolate: for I say to you, you shall see me no more till you say, 'Blessed is he who comes in the name of the Lord.'" Matthew 23:39.

Whatever you are going through, cultivate peace and joy. The joy of the Lord is your strength. My most cherished saints are Samuel and Sarah Muhoro, who were students of my father. Their dreadful episode occurred in the dark and cold night. The persecutors broke into their home and demanded that they deny Christ. When they refused, the killers started butchering Samuel. Sarah was so filled with peace and joy she started smiling. The killers stopped killing the husband and then cut Sarah's small finger and rebuked her, "Why are you smiling at us! Don't you know that we are murderers?"

"I know," Sarah responded, "but God loves you."

So Sarah's peaceful demeanor diffused their anger. They stop killing Samuel but took all the blankets. Sarah said to them as they were leaving, "Folks! Don't forget we have children. We need some blankets." They then threw some blankets to them and said, "Be praying for us."

As a prophet of the Most High, remember his encouraging words: "Be still and know that I am God." Psalm 46:10.
"Cast your burden upon the Lord and He will sustain you." Psalm 55:22. Own the great promises. Remember the words of our precious Savior, "Blessed are you when they revile you and persecute you, and say all kinds of evil against you falsely for my sake. Rejoice and be exceedingly glad for great is your reward in heaven, for so they persecuted the prophets who were before you." Matthew 5:11-12.

YOU ARE WRESTLING WITH UNREGENERATES AND BACKSLIDERS

Do you understand that you are wrestling with bishops, lay leader who are not born again or backsliders? These are people who are at the church but are not in the church. They have form, but no substance. They are Christian by name and formality, but have locked the Spirit of God out of their lives. They are with the people who are in the Kingdom of God, but they are not in the Kingdom and cannot see the Kingdom of God. They are very much like unconverted Nicodemus. You remember the story. When he went to Jesus by night and started praising Jesus. Jesus told him the truth about himself and about the Kingdom of God. Jesus emphatically told Nicodemus, "Most assuredly, I say to you, unless one is born again, he cannot see the kingdom of God."

So do realize that your flock includes sheep (the born-again) and wolves. You have wolves in all church strata from lay reader to archbishop. But you also have the children of light in all church positions. We understand the mind-set of both groups because we were all born in sin. The apostle Paul put it this way, "For us ourselves were also foolish, disobedient, deceived, serving various lusts and pleasures, living in malice and envy, hateful and hating one another. But when the kindness of the love of God our Savior toward man appeared, not by work of righteousness which we have done, but according to his mercy: he saved us, through the washing of regeneration and renewing of the Holy Spirit, whom he poured out on us abundantly through Jesus Christ our Savior. That having been justified by his grace we should become heirs according to the hope of eternal life. Titus 3:3-7. Here Paul is calling a spade a spade. If you are going through it this time, you may discover that all those who are waging war with you are in the same basket. They are deceivers and deceived. On one occasion, the person who falsely accused me to the ecclesiastical authority had been challenged by the sermon I had delivered about regeneration. I still remember the anointing I had on that Sunday, which was following by Episcopal visitation. This lady lied and said that I was Africanizing them. After this she was so tortured by her conscience, she called me the following day and said, "Father, forgive me for lying to the bishop about you. I have a clean heart but a dirty mouth." My answer was,

"Could you please pick up the phone and tell the bishop that you lied to him? "She responded, "I don't have the courage to do that."

Then the following day I found a gift in my office from my accuser. But my dear bishop was more interested in lies than in truth. He so regarded the lie as absolute truth that he laid off the only black priest he had in the diocese to save his flock from "African-ness and accent." The underlying issue was being in flesh and bearing the fruits of the flesh.

If you are in Spirit, you have no problem distinguishing the unregenerate from generated. The life of a slave to sin is characterized by foolishness, disobedience, deception, lust, malice, envy, hatred, anger, and jealousy. The regenerated bear the fruit of the spirit, which are love, joy, peace, long suffering, kindness, goodness, faithfulness, gentleness, and self-control. J.C. Ryle, one of the most spiritual Anglican bishops, wrote about eight marks of the new birth.

1. *The first mark of the new birth is whoever is born of God doth not commit sin.*

"Whosoever is born of God sinneth not." 1 John 5:18. This according to Ryle this means "He no longer takes a light and cool and easy way to sin.He hates it and abhors it, and desires to cut off it's roots and branches with his whole heart and mind and soul and strength."

2. *The second mark is faith in Christ.*

Whoever believes that Jesus is the Christ is born of God. 1 John 5:1.

Ryle states, "I do not mean by this a general, vague sort of faith which the devil possesses. I mean rather that (conviction) which comes over a man when he is really convinced of his own guilt and unworthiness and sees that Christ alone can be his Savior." I should admit that I have never seen someone who is in Christ waging war with the faithful minister of the Gospel. So those who do are thorns in the flesh, "Christians without Christ." They are a part of our mission field and this is why we have to forgive them because tomorrow they may be convinced by the Spirit of their sins.

3. *The third mark of the new birth is holiness.*

The apostle John tells us that everyone who practices righteousness is born of Him. He who is born of God keeps him, and the wicked one does not touch him. I John 2:29, 5:18. Those who are in Christ are not led by the devil but by the Spirit of God. They therefore work with but not against the priest.

4. *The fourth mark of the new birth is spiritual mindedness.*

Since they are risen with Christ they "seek those things which are above." They set their affection on things that are above, not on the things that are on earth. These lovely Christians have no desire to complain about the pastor because he is earning more money than they. They couldn't care less about a typographic error in the bulletin. They may be liturgical, but they don't worship the liturgy.

5. *The fifth mark of the new birth is victory over the world.*

For whoever is born of God overcomes the world. And this is the victory that has overcome the world, our faith. Ryle put it this way, "The spiritual man is no longer like a dead fish floating with the stream of earthly opinion; he is ever pressing upwards, looking unto Jesus in spite of all opposition. He has overcome the world." So whatever you are going through, remember that you are a winner. Own God's great promises: "Fear not, I have redeemed you; I have called you by name, you are mine. When you pass through the waters I will be with you; and through the rivers they will not overflow you. When you walk through the fire, you shall not be burned, nor shall the flame scorch you. "For I am the Lord your God, the Holy One of Israel, your Savior." Isaiah 43:1b-2. So if God is for us who can be against us? In all things we are more than conquerors through Him who loved us. We are indeed winners.

6. *The sixth mark of the new birth is meekness.*

Remember it is by pride that the angels fell and became devils. Some of the people who are antagonistic to the priest were people who had seen the light. But when God exalted them, they reciprocated with pride and became autocratic. This was what happened to Saul, the first king of Israel. He started well, but eventually he fell out of grace and became ruthless to the very people who were fighting for him, including his son Jonathan, and David his son-in-law. Some of the church leaders were elected by the people of God because of their grace and fruitful ministry. But when they acquired money and power, they became corrupt and empty wells.

If you have gone through it, you will agree with me that the people who belittled you were arrogant. But when you are going through it, connect with meek people. You will find in the church family those who are humble and are more concerned about repenting of their own sin than in projecting them to their spiritual leader. These people have no time to find fault with others or be a busybody about their neighbors. Most clergy will tell you that the very first person who came to them when they arrived in the parish was also the very person who started poisoning the body of Christ against the minister.

7. *The seventh mark of the new birth is a great delight in all means of grace.*

I still remember what happened to me when I committed myself to Christ at the age of 15. Things which never mattered became most important: church worship, Bible study, Christian fellowship, and volunteering for anything that the priest asked me to do. Being in the company of the people of God became as sweet as honey. As a newborn baby, I had a great desire for the sincere milk of the Word. Those who are born again have a give and take attitude. They draw the best from the clergy and the church family. When they come to church, they are interested in particles of gold rather than sand. They will always find something that will draw them closer to God. They attend church services and special events regularly. They can benefit spiritually from the gathering of two or three as they can from five thousand. This is why you, as a priest, must value their presence even if they may be one or two. Remember that they don't worship numbers, but God. Like David they will tell you: "The law that you give means more to me than all the money in the world." Psalm 119:72 (GNB).

8. *The eighth mark of the new birth is love toward others.*

As the Apostle John admonishes: "Beloved, let us love one another, for love is of God, and everyone who loves is born of God and knows God. Those who give you a hard time in ministry are also people who have locked God outside of their lives. And the message that they need is that which Jesus gave to Nicodemus: "Unless one is born of water and the Spirit he cannot enter the Kingdom of God." Don't be discouraged, however, if you don't succeed in winning them for Christ. Remember Jesus, who is God-man, had Judas for three years. And Judas chose the way of damnation. So you are just a messenger. You are not a messiah.

IT IS WAR BETWEEN LIGHT AND DARKENESS

Being regenerated means that you are a bearer of Christ. You are Christopher. You abide in the one who said, "I am the light of the world, He who follows me will not walk in darkness but have the light of life." You are a child of God in a special way. You are saved. David would put it this way: "The Lord is my light and my salvation, whom shall I fear?"

By being the bearer of light, you scare the children of darkness. When you scare them, they hate you. The light in you scares them because their deeds are evil.

Being a child of light implies doing things in a right way and in God's way. You follow the footsteps of your Master who said, "I am the way, and the truth and life." You take a higher way that enables you to operate in a higher energy system. You possess the keys to success: forgiving, giving, and thanksgiving. You are also fully convinced that the **will of God** will never take you where the **grace of God** will not protect you.

This high energy system does not allow negative emotions such as jealousy and fear. Children of darkness, on the other hand, are dominated by a lower frequency system of negativity, which "suck up the energy." This has a negative effect on their activities. This will turn them to a "C" or "F" while you are an "A" in your performance. This provokes their jealousy and gives them the desire to destroy you. If you are suffering for being a child of light, don't put your light under the bushel. Keep on shining. Remember the word of the Apostle John, "In Him was life, and that life was the light of men and the light shines in the darkness and the darkness has not overcome it." You are not a victim, you are a victor. In the deepest sense the darkness is the absence of God. It is absence of Universal Energy. But as a child of God you possess this enormous energy. It was this energy that broke the chain that had bound Peter in prison and forced the prison doors open. It is the same light that guided the Israelites in the wilderness. It was the same light that guided the Wise Men to the baby Jesus. And it is the same light that will lead you to your eternal home. When you select nonphysical light, you see things through the authentically empowered rank in creation. You then have more ability to see without obstruction, more ability to live in love and wisdom, and more ability and desire to help others to see and experience the light. The light will lead you to a realm where you will experience perfect peace, perfect love, and perfect joy.

CHAPTER TWENTY-SEVEN

CONCLUSION

In conclusion we are urging you to be starting your day with prayer, and reading the Word of God. If you are married do this with your spouse. Use the word of God as your mission statement. Being international my wife and I have several mission statements Mary and I start the day by singing three songs which are a part of our mission statement. We sing three songs to worship God who has revealed as one in three, we sang in three languages: Kikuyu, Swahili, and English. You can also compose your own songs. When I was a teenager and undergoing through the persecution of deprivation of food. I was living with my uncle and my anti was making and selling illegal bear, but the Holy Spirit would not allow me to participate in this business. And for three years, I serviced with a cup of tea in the morning and a small portion of food for supper. Yet this was my most joyous years and I was doing street evangelism. This time, the Lord gives me new songs. The first song was:

The greatest treasure
The greatest joy;
The greatest peace;
Is Christ the Lord

Prof. John Gatungu Githiga

You who are chained

By your sin and excuses

Come to Jesus,

And He will save you.

To motivate myself for daily ministry, I sung:

One step to heaven is required.

One step to heaven is required every day.

One step to heaven is required.

By one step I mean preaching to one person. And I was motivated to reach out to so many people who included African, European and Asians. When my brother Habel joined me three years later we teamed together. And we were always filled with overflowing joy.

When I became so thin, I had a song for my body:

This body we have is not perfect.

It is made of dust.

But it should not keep us from heaven.

Even thou live or die we must.

From dust it was made by our Father.

Dust it shall become.

This body we have is not perfect.

For us or anyone.

Now those who will trust the Father.

He will rice to be.

In wonderful,

Perfect new bodies

With him eternally.

Hence, my beloved, motive yourself with songs and Psalms. And know that whatever you do for the Lord is not in vain. My greatest joy is that both my aunt and Uncle committed themselves to Christ. My brother Habel, who is gifted in winning the soul, brought them to Christ and they left bear business and became landlord and goal keeper. They were very active in the Roman Catholic Church. So, my beloved keep on serving the Lord no matter what.

You can also use the mission statement from the people of God to motivate yourself. As I have mentioned, Mary and I have drowned from international Christian bodies: When were in courtship we adopted Mothers Union mission statement: "**I can do allthings through Christ who strengthens me**." Also being Church Army Captain, we were Motivated by their motto: "**Fight a good fight**." And also, being officers of Girls and Boys Brigade: we have "**sure and steadfast**." From BB and "**seek and followChrist**."From GB. My Mission statement is:

God give me work.

Till my life shall end.

And life, till my work is done.

Finally, if you have the goat head, commit yourselves to Christ who says: "I stand at the door and knock, if anyone hears my voice and open the door; I will come in and dine with him and he with me. Revelation 3:20. Christ is closer to you than you nose is closer to your mouth. When he comes in, he will give you a new heart: This is what the word of God says about the new life in Christ: "whatever is true, whatever is noble, whatever is right, whatever is pure, whatever is lovely, whatever is admirable- if anything is excellent or praiseworthy-Think about such things." Philippians 4:8-9. You will indeed bear much fruits- fruits which will remain forever. You will be God's delight for you will bear the fruit of the Spirit which is: love, joy, peace, patience, kindness, goodness, faithfulness, gentleness and self-control.

Leadership With Goat Head

Prof. John Gatungu Githiga

www.ingramcontent.com/pod-product-compliance
Lightning Source LLC
LaVergne TN
LVHW091048100526
838202LV00077B/3096